EIGHT FOR IMMORTALITY

W. H. Davies

EIGHT FOR IMMORTALITY

BY

RICHARD CHURCH

Essay Index Reprint Series

BOOKS FOR LIBRARIES PRESS
FREEPORT, NEW YORK

STANDARD BOOK NUMBER:

8369-1204-7

LIBRARY OF CONGRESS CATALOG CARD NUMBER:

70-90623

PRINTED IN THE UNITED STATES OF AMERICA

To the memory of W. H. Davies, a friend
whose death in 1940 has given an additional
significance to the first of these essays.

CONTENTS

Acknowledgments are due to the editor of the *Fortnightly Review*, at whose instigation these essays were written for his magazine.

Thanks are also due to Messrs Jonathan Cape for supplying copies of Dame Laura Knight's portrait of W. H. Davies and the photograph of Mr Robert Frost; to Messrs Faber & Faber for the photograph of Mr Walter de la Mare, and also to Messrs Elliott & Fry for that of Mr T. S. Eliot; to Messrs Macmillan for the photographs of Mr Edmund Blunden and Mr W. B. Yeats; to Messrs A. P. Watt and Mr Douglas Glass for the photograph of Mr Robert Graves; and to Mr Howard Coster for the photograph of Miss V. Sackville-West

ix

W. H. DAVIES: THE MAN AND HIS WORK

Mr W. H. Davies has just published another little book of poems, called The Loneliest Mountain.[1] At the beginning he puts a note which says that 'whatever happens, the present book ends my career as a living author.' I recall, however, that he said much the same thing in 1910, when he published his fourth book of verse and called it Farewell to Poesy. He was forty years old then. He is sixty-nine to-day. There is thus less reason to doubt his present resignation.

But I do doubt it, for I know the man. I cannot say, as Mr Shaw said in 1907 when he wrote his famous preface to Mr Davies's Autobiography of a Super-tramp, a book which is now safely a classic, that 'I hasten to protest at the outset that I have no personal knowledge of the incorrigible super - tramp who wrote this amazing book.' So what I have to say here is likely to be coloured by my admiration and affection for this remarkable man, and I had better explain at the beginning what I owe to him, so that for the moment I can forget it. To talk of one's affec-tions is to dispel them, at least temporarily (as

---

[1] Cape. 3s. 6d.

1

William Blake said), and that is what I want to do now so that I can write of his poetry without bias.

I first met that poetry in 1911, when I was lent a volume called *Nature Poems*.   It happened at a moment in a youngster's life when he is very exalted by his youthful discoveries in the new field of literature. That is a period of magnificent intolerance.   Only the best will do; Milton, Spenser, and the other immortals who have just begun to make the new-comer's acquaintance.   So when I was offered poetry by a living man I felt a certain condescension.

How quickly that condescension was dispelled! I fell under the spell of Mr Davies's simplicity at once. I have remained under it ever since.   But more of that later.   I want first to speak of the man.   I met him in 1918, a few months after my first book of verses had been published by his publisher, Fifield. It was a happy coincidence for me, because the publisher showed my book to Mr Davies and in due course I received a post card, written in a script that looked like a collection of blackthorn buds.   It invited me to call and see him in his rooms near the British Museum.   It explained that I must knock loudly with the knocker, because the bell was out of order and that owing to the war it could not be put right.

I followed these instructions, and thus began an acquaintance which developed into a friendship. And one cannot discuss friendships easily in public. I found a small but sturdy man, who because of the accident described in his autobiography, walked round the room with a hopping limp. His face was a warm brown, his suit was brown, and his eyes were large, shining, and still more brown. He was like a bird; a sparrow, a thrush, a nightingale; a touch of wildness, a brilliance of vision, a shyness, a voice rich and musical.

He gave me tea, and talked kindly about my first effort as an artist in verse-making. I listened to what he said, and some of it has stuck: especially one thing. It was this. ' Never lose your enthusiasm.' He then went on to speak of the brilliant beginners, with scholarship and much more at their command, whom he had seen degenerate into disillusioned literary men, bored by everything and especially by literature. He warned me not to become one of those. It sounded a simple enough axiom then. I have realized since how much wisdom lay behind it, and how difficult it is to live up to it. It has been a sort of life-line to me, and it will be until I and my enthusiasm are removed elsewhere by Time, that greatest of all Enthusiasts.

I could tell a thousand and one stories which would throw light on this man and his character, both as friend and poet. They would all be benevolent ones, for I have never known him do a mean thing. Even in his animosities and shrewdness he has the quality of innocence; the quality which is the mainspring of his work. Of all the many writers whom I have met since—he was the first—I have met none in whom the man and his work are so completely identified. Davies's poetry is Davies. The appearance, the colour, tone, movement, joy, and fear of the man are exactly those found in the verse. This is an important matter for a critic to note. I suppose, from what evidence I can find from contemporary records, that Wordsworth was the same. It means that Davies is a *complete* poet; not a clever literary man. He is a unit; limited to himself; and that self is a singer. The knowledge and wisdom which he brings to the singing are restricted to his own experience. He explores it as completely as a sparrow explores a patch of a stable yard.

My first conception of the man was of a being endowed with an extraordinary kindness. It showed in his eloquent eyes, his whimsical smile which caused his strong mouth (the mouth of an old salt) to break into a smile so that his dry, shag-cured lips almost parted, but not quite. And from that not-quite a little bubbling sound of mirth, sheer delight, escaped. As I got to know the man better, I learned how much that delight signified; the generosity behind it.

It became a habit for me to go to tea with him once a week. I always found him waiting with an egg which he put on to boil as soon as I arrived. He said that I was too thin, and needed extra nourishment. A year or so later, when I called as usual, I found one day a visitor there. It was Roger Ingpen, then a publisher. The result of that meeting was my second book of verse. A long time after I learned from Roger Ingpen that if it had been necessary, Mr Davies had offered to finance the volume from his very meagre income and Civil List pension. Events like that are epochs in one's life. The reader can understand why I want to put such things aside for a moment, while I try to assess the value of this body of poetry which Mr Davies says has now come to an end. I still don't believe him. I know that as long as he lives, and can look out of a window, or stare into a fire, even if from the bed of a man crippled with age and infirmity, there will ensue some songs about light and warmth and all that they symbolize for this man gifted with an infinite genius for

B

gratitude. He knows this too. He says, in his valedictory volume:

> How softly now my Days go by—
> How quietly the Moments glide!
> Yet, underneath, I feel the rush
> Of a swifter, stronger tide.
>
> And though my Days glide softly by,
> I ache from the throbs and fears
> Of a terrible tide that, underneath,
> Is carrying off my Years!

And I must quote another proof, if proof be needed.

> Be damned, you cheeks, be damned and sink;
> Body, bend double, sag and shrink;
> Go dry, poor Skin, go thick and dry;
> Sweet light, collect in neither eye;
> Body, be damned—shall I not find
> Your faults redeemed by my unfailing Mind?
>
> A Mind that's strong enough to bear
> A Dream-child every day of the year;
> A Spirit full of young desire,
> With growing pains, to reach up higher—
> Is there no joy for men that think?
> Body, be damned, bend double, sag and shrink!
> Fools have their second childhood, but the Great
> Still keep their first, and have no second state.

I have quoted that poem because it takes us much further in our estimate of this poet's life-work. You see that he says in these latter days what he said to me personally twenty-one years ago. This is an example of what I mean by the man and his work being in identity. In telling me to keep my enthusiasm he was expressing the same conviction as where he says, as a poet, that ' the Great still keep their first childhood, and have no second state.' For Mr Davies, childhood is the symbol of enthusiasm, the immediate curiosity, the passion of interest, the complete absorption of self in the discovery of something. Davies the poet is a child still. He has a child's particularity which is yet such an oddly unscientific power, because it has no sense of relationship or classification. Davies the poet is still a child in his attitude to Nature because he never wants to codify it, or generalize into principles what he sees, hears, and smells. Compare, for example, his knowledge of trees with that of Tennyson. One could almost make botanical drawings from Tennyson's references to trees and flowers. But with Davies you will find that his reference is usually to a few generalized types; the cherry-tree, the plum-tree, the oak. But I doubt if on his daily walks he will be able to, or care to, distinguish one from the other, except during the flowering season. It is the same with the animals and birds whom he loves so much.

He loves them too as a child loves them; with capital
letters.   Search his poems and you will find a thousand references to the robin, that ' feathered bully '
the sparrow, or to the nightingale with ' the moon's
white beams across her throat.'   But that will be
about all the natural history in which Mr Davies cares
to indulge.   It is an astonishing thing how a poet,
so genuinely enraptured with beast, bird, and plant,
can go all his life singing about them, yet never be
curious to know their variations, their specific habits
and qualities.   The poetaster, with woolly mind,
might remain thus addicted to generalizations, but
nobody would read his verse.   We read Mr Davies,
however, and we recognize true poetry, that strange
and exciting power, in his lyrics with their eighteenth-
century habit of apostrophizing things and labelling
them with capital letters.   As he says to-day,

> I have no ears or eyes
> For either bird or flower,

but even so he conjures a world of minute and factual
happenings down to the reader's hand; and a shy,
elusive world it is too.   His lyrics give us the same
feeling, that sort of skin-caress delight, which we
experience when we persuade a robin to come and
feed from our hand, or when——as happened once to

him—a butterfly alights on the pencil with which
we are writing.

It is therefore absurd to call Davies a nature poet.
Nature poets, with their meticulous catalogues—
such as John Clare gives us—can be bores. Davies,
with his handful of references which he repeats
again and again, is never a bore. On the contrary,
he puts a sort of enchantment upon us, just as a
thrush does when we hear it in autumn prophesying
of next year's spring. The emotion is a kind of
nostalgia, a harking back to the morning of life,
of time, the lost realm of innocence, where everything is wonder, and nothing is knowledge.

How then does he manage to do this? We see
how limited he is in what he says. A technical
examination of his verse further reveals how limited
he is in how he says it. His devices have all been
used before by the Caroline minor poets, and by the
fanciful verse-makers of the eighteenth century. Yet
Davies can be as playful and fanciful as he likes, and
he catches our hearts.

My fancy loves to play with Clouds
That hour by hour can change Heaven's face;
For I am sure of my delight,
In green or stony place.

You see the vagueness of it, and the Augustan habit

of those capital letters.　But you will also see in that verse—an early one taken from his first selected volume of poems—the explanation of his power over the reader.　'For I am sure of my delight in green or stony place' is an absolute truth which defines the man and the poet.　It identifies them too, so that the two become one, and remain one throughout the long life of this remarkable personality. Even in misery, pain, and rage, Davies is sure of his delight.　He distils that aromatic drop of song from his surroundings, though he may be sitting in the hold of a sailing ship, tending seasick cattle; or lying in a Canadian hospital, in the casualty ward, after his foot has been cut off by a locomotive.

I spoke of rage.　That brings us to another side of this poet.　It is a side which has also found expression in a simple prose that earned the praise of Shaw, who said of the *Autobiography of a Super-tramp*, that 'this book, which is printed as it was written, without any academic corrections from the point of view of the Perfect Commercial Letter Writer, is worth reading by literary experts for its style alone.' It is worth reading because it burns with rage, a fine, clear rage as lucid as his delight, as free as his joy.　But here again the emotion is not detailed, is not worked up into a political or social principle.

A few tramps, a few hungry old beggar women, a cheated prostitute, a brutally used child, a tortured animal; these are the material with which Davies feeds his divine rage, and which are sufficient to make him realize that what he sees here on earth merits some thought about an afterworld, a presiding God, and a personal soul within himself. It is significant that his first book, published from a Walworth doss-house, was called *The Soul's Destroyer*. Since then he has never ceased to sing, between his moods of sheer delight in momentary lovely things, of the fatal cruelty of man, of beast and bird, of the waves of the sea, which with a blind indifference pursue a destiny of destruction that Mr Davies is not scientist enough to pretend to understand or explain, but which he can expose in songs as excoriating and horrifying as the events they portray.

> I saw that woman go from place
> To place, hungry for her child's face;
> I heard her crying, crying, crying;
> Then, in a flash! saw the Sea trying
> With savage joy, and efforts wild,
> To smash his rocks with a dead child.

But in this outcry of pain there is the same detachment as in his delight. It is the detachment of the child, the bewilderment that is also an ecstasy, the fear that is also enthusiasm. Yes, enthusiasm. And that is where we started from. But that is where we always come to with this man's work. It forms a complete sphere, a little world of its own. That is why it is likely to take its place in the cosmos of English poetry, a permanent planet.

Most great writers enter the world backwards. They are people who have a long journey before them, a life-journey in the land of self-expression, and they linger at the outset, gazing back at the fields and roofs of literature, where they first fed, and saw, and felt. Those are the moments of ' sedulous ' imitation, as Stevenson called them. Later, they have to turn and face their own experience, a narrow and forbidding path, in comparison with the wide view they are leaving behind.

It is characteristic of Walter de 'la Mare that he should have been conscious, even in those early stages of his travel, that he was thus walking semi-Janus-wise. He even made copy out of his apprenticeship, his period of sedulousness, and wrote a prose book called *Henry Brocken*, in which the characters are not reflections from people in his own world, but reconjurings of names famous in fiction; Rosinante, Annabel Lee, Jane Eyre, and the like. He said, with an artful confidingness: ' Some perhaps who read of the personages that cross these pages are already familiar with them face to face. They will have nothing but contempt for such poor shadows of them as I shall conjure up.'

But what is interesting to the critic is that readers did not have contempt for those 'poor shadows.' Indeed, they were fascinated, horrified by them. Mr de la Mare's already alert consciousness — that tool which a creative writer must never allow to be blunted—was skilfully at work. He was concentrating and manipulating all the disadvantages of youth and its sparse experience in life, and he was making a beautiful and original work of art of what, if allowed to remain unexpressed, would have been the usual diluent in his work for many years to come.

And it is to be noted that this book, and all his work preceding it, was written under the pseudonym of 'Walter Ramal,' which is another deliberate back-to-front stance.

But a victory, especially a quick victory, has its dangers. Mr de la Mare evaded the long years of literary allusions, imitations, and echoes which most writers have to pass through. But in evading them by so successful a device, he became somewhat the victim of his success, and made a habit of the backward search, knowing his own skill in utilizing it. Had he not been so skilful an artist, this habit might have circumscribed his genius. He might have become 'a poet of childhood'; a dreadful fate. It was a narrow escape, even so. Let us see how he escaped.

Hs is explicit on the matter. In his Introduction to Mr Frank Kendon's The Small Years (a book which in my view is one of the most beautiful records of childhood in our language), he says:

Nor is it merely the plums of childhood that in memory taste so sweet. A curious delicious flavour may haunt even its duff. The commonest objects —a cupboard, a mug, a slice of cake, a door bell, an old rocking-horse, a picture on a wall, the light reflected from snow, an old man's beard, his alpaca coat, the white of his eyes as he knelt praying— such things as these were somehow more themselves and therefore more enthralling. And it is not merely that growing older has bestowed on them a glamour evoked by time, envy, and regret. Like runes scribbled on some grey old mouldering pre-historic stone, they had a secret meaning, though what precisely that meaning was we may not be able to say.

The key to his escape lies in that last sentence. Throughout his work, and amid all its variety, Mr de la Mare has kept an unwavering preoccupation with the riches of childhood. It may be this element in his vitality which gives him a certain affinity with the seventeenth-century poet Henry Vaughan, also an

explorer in the same territory.   But whereas Vaughan
saw it with a Silurian, a Celtic eye, Mr de la Mare sees it
with more edge to his vision, a keener melancholy,
a touch of Latin madness or excitement.   It is to be
remembered that he is of Huguenot stock.

So here we see him definitely exploiting his preoccupation, and thereby setting his style and his
field of interests.   He began at an early stage to see
the world around him; of nature, of man, and even
of God, as a sort of cryptic writing, a code message
condensing the realities of a more remote, and in-
finitely most vast and august, as well as more terrible
universe which lies behind the quicksilver of the
mirror, within the candle-flame, under the rhythm of
the blood, and beyond the fence of logic.   So in
looking back to childhood, he is not narrowing down
his range of vision.   He is intensifying it, guiding
it through a sort of ravine in the certainty that by
this path he may find his way to that universe of
realities.

Thus both his initial success, and the subsequent
danger, are re-exploited, and the artist emerges
mature.   De la Mare's thumb-mark is on all he does.
His idiosyncrasy can be recognized no matter what
medium he is working in.   And that is the sign of
maturity.   He has now reached such sureness of his

own estate that he can dare to intellectualize it—
during moments of certainty and comfort—without
the fear of breaking through its fabric. This process
is a necessary one for every artist. It is the means
by which, during his ' off-moments,' he sharpens
his tools and perfects his technique. De la Mare is
never afraid of, nor tired of doing so. In his latest
book, the massive anthology Behold, this Dreamer, he
has a long prefatory essay, and in that essay lies a
footnote which I must quote entire because of its
bearing on my exploration of his development, and
also because it is an example of his technical equip-
ment. For here is a prose paragraph which is flaw-
less in its cadence. Read it aloud, and note the
swing of the sentences, the cunning pauses of the
parentheses, the gradual increase of volume until
the last word ' introspection ' rings home like a
resolutory chord at the end of a fugue by Bach.
Such prose puts de la Mare among the masters:
Sir Thomas Browne, Swift, and De Quincey (though
this last has a more subtle use of the colon than
Mr de la Mare, or indeed than any other English
writer). Here is the paragraph:

This ' Unconscious ' (so far as it is practicable) is
now being actively explored—and the novice should
fear to tread. It is a convenient but unanimating

term for the reservoir of *elixir vitae* from which,
throughout the waking day and at every moment of
dream, is being drawn up into consciousness, even
though it may serve its purpose unperceived, the
imagery of recognition, recollection, and re-creation.
The submerged portion of an iceberg is the commonest metaphor for it; but that of an archipelago of
humanity whose myriad island peaks are connected
under the sea may be nearer the mark. Intuition
in part depends on its resources; and, past calculating,
the faculty or poise or, rather, state of the mind
which we call the Imagination. Its influence may
be the cause of what fascinates or repels us in a
fellow creature; and for the 'mystery,' l'inconnu, which
Man in his devotion seeks in vain to fathom in
Woman. Its precious metals glint out of the quartz
of the confirmed 'character'; it inspires the con-
summate actor; and more or less controls the born
demagogue. It can be the devil in human affairs.
Yet it nourishes the flower of mystical contemplation.
It is the Hesperides of the Muses. As the utterance of
verbal sounds with the vocal organs has its own
sensuous aesthetic reactions, and facial expression in-
tensifies the emotions it represents, so every natural
posture of the body is the outcome and revelation
of a state of the mind and of the unconscious mind.
Even in the merest novice mimicry of the attitudes
of the Buddha will induce some trace of the spiritual
attitudes which they represent—a kind of empathy;
and any true understanding of a piece of statuary is
at least in part dependent on a similar intuitive process. What—in any original enterprise of mind or
spirit—can man achieve, indeed, unaided by the re-

viving waters of this unplumbable well? A well
lapped in darkness—and every metaphor is only a
makeshift—into which we can peer only with the
aid of a feeble taper, introspection.

You see from this paragraph, this footnote thrown
in as an afterthought, what have been de la Mare's
activities since the Walter Ramal days. He is still
Walter Ramal, but with the consciousness of his
backward glance intensified by the science of effort,
of patient exploration. In between those moments
of incandescent mood when his mind is in creative
labour, he has been at work trying to find a rational
explanation of what he has made, and of the vision
which urged him to make it. He has been compelled to this by that ever-nagging sense of dis-
honesty from which the creative artist suffers about
his work. He strives and strives; yet by some queer
chemistry the permanent and living poem is born
out of a sleight of hand as it were at the side of that
strife. So the resting craftsman tries to fit the two
gestures into one, to associate them from a single
impulse, knowing that so long as his effort at creation
remains slightly different from the actual movement
of creation, he can never be sure of himself, or of
the physical validity of his work. As he says:

A poem, however ethereal its contents may be,

has been packed in a material verbal basket, has been distilled into a transparent phial. Yet its symbols carry it as lightly and unobtrusively as a rose carries its dew, or an animal its nature. It therefore has a formal and finished loveliness which few dreams can achieve, but which even dreams may occasionally bestow. It is exquisitely at liberty in a cage of words which it is not only a joy to examine, but which is as necessary to all that it holds for our delight as the skin of a cherry is for the security of its stone.

All his life as a writer, de la Mare has been occupied with this tremendous effort to reconcile the elusiveness of his sources of interest with the solidity of his medium of words. In this he is no different from other poets. The difference is in the strategy by which he first set about the task, and the results achieved. I have tried to show how that initial strategy by its immediate success also fixed upon him a habit of thought and vision which has helped to make his mature work what it is, and to emphasize its distinction both in subject and expression. No other poet is so clearly betrayed by his phrase, his technical devices. Every sensibility which marks de la Mare's odd way of looking at life as it were in the reflection of time (like his hero in The Return) has an immediate hand in the forming of his rhythms, his almost private emphases, his com-

Walter de la Mare

pletely habitual inversions. One critic, Mr Forrest
Reid, has pointed out that so strong has been the
sensibility that the effect on the poetry has been to
create a mannerism frequently in danger of self-parody.
In the slighter poems this weakness is often apparent.

And the danger does not end there, in technical
matters. The whole temper of his work, which I
believe has been partly conditioned by that almost
facile early maturing, is toward an oblique attack
upon present experience. Thus his prose is never
colloquial, and never contemporary. It belongs
where he, by temperament, belongs, to the late
seventeenth century. It is so slow, so richly weighted
in movement, like the cadences of Taylor or Browne.
At first, coming to it from modern utility prose, the
reader is baffled, and inclined to murmur querulously
about its being too literary. But soon its magic begins
to work, compelling a discipline upon the mind.
He sees the terrible reality and fearlessness of the
poet's mind. Here is an example. ' Why all this
sleep?—seven, eight, nine, ten hours perhaps—with
a living to make, work to be done, thoughts to be
thought, obligations to keep, a soul to save, friends
to refrain from losing, pleasure to seek, and that
prodigious host of activities known as life? '

There is nothing he does not explore in this
c

inquiry into the permutations of sleep; its depth,
its range, its perversions. He says: ' For my own
part, I have spent in sleep a far more active and
adventurous existence than has been my outward
lot in the waking day. What that may foreshadow
who can say? The fortunate perhaps may follow
the liveliest careers in both. But the precise relation
between the life of the imagination and that in the
external world is obscure.' De la Mare has tried in
his work to shape a refractometer for gauging that
obscurity.

But here the remarkable alertness of this poet's
consciousness again shows itself. Out of all his
weaknesses—and the greatest of poets has as much
weakness as he is human—de la Mare makes artistic
capital. No writer has ever been more awake to
the dangers besetting his path. He even enjoys it,
and dances near the brink of the precipices which he
sees in his own nature.

O brave adventure; Ay, at danger slake
Thy thirst, lest life in thee should, sickening, quail;
But not toward nightmare goad a mind awake,
Nor to forbidden horizons bend thy sail—
Seductive outskirts whence in trance prolonged
Thy gaze, at stretch of what is sane-secure,
Dreams out on steeps by shapes demoniac thronged
And vales wherein alone the dead endure.

Nectarous those flowers, yet with venom sweet.
Thick-juiced with poison hang those fruits that shine
Where sick phantasmal moonbeams brood and beat,
And dark imaginations ripe the vine.
Bethink thee: every enticing league thou wend
Beyond the mark where life its bound hath set
Will lead thee at length where human pathways end
And the dark enemy spreads his maddening net.

Throughout his work he refers, sometimes at length as in this quotation, sometimes in a single epithet, to the danger of his queer backward-walking progress through life and through his personal experience in this world, and even in possible other worlds co-existent with it. He see his acute sensibility tending to a sort of inaction. He sees himself dreading to touch anything directly — even life itself, lest he should send it crashing into ruins. And he deplores his own remoteness, the result of that dread; and the deploration sets an overtone to his poetry, and affects its rhythm, giving it a certain frantic, dancing-in-the-distance quality. Not only in his verse, but also in his most realistic novels, this quality is perceptible. In one of his stories, At First Sight, he betrays himself in a casual description of a clergy-man who ' had done excellent, if rather active, work in the parish '! Note that antinomy.

But that inaction becomes a strength, a double

strength. First, it pacifies his inward vision, th
tortured scene of self.

> I sit alone,
> And clear thoughts move in me,
> Pictures, now near, now far,
> Of transient fantasy.
> Happy I am, at peace
> In my own company.
>
> Yet life is a dread thing, too,
> Dark with horror and fear.
> Beauty's fingers grow cold,
> Sad cries I hear,
> Death with a stony gaze
> Is ever near.
>
> Lost in myself I hide
> From the cold unknown:
> Lost, like a world cast forth
> Into space star-sown:
> And the songs of the morning are stilled,
> And delight in them flown.

It is a sad pacification, perhaps, but it is effective,
and it leads to his second source of strength. It
makes him see with that fierce intensity by which
the mind's eye is lighted at times of crisis; it gives
him perpetually the vividness of grief, the clarity of
fever, which his art enables him to utilize without
despair or delirium. Look how he describes a
winter morning.

Already dawn was clear and high in the sky,
already the first breezes were moving in the mists;
and breathed chill, as if it were the lingering darkness itself on my cheeks. The air was cold, yet with
a fresh, faint sweetness. The snow lay crisp across
its perfect surface, mounded softly over the gorse-
bushes, though here and there a spray of parched
blossom yet protruded from its cowl. Flaky
particles of ice floated invisible in the air. I called
out with pleasure to see the little ponds where the
snow had been blown away from the black ice. I
saw on the bushes too the webs of spiders stretched
from thorn to thorn, and festooned with crystals
of hoar-frost. I turned and counted as far as I
could my footsteps leading back to the house, which
lay roofed in gloomy pallor, dim and obscured in
in the darkened west.

What a strange agony it is, this conflict within
him, of clarity in near objects against an ever
receding horizon. You see how he is forced to
repudiate the pleasure and to retrace his ' footsteps
leading back to the house.' But what house is that?
It is the house where the poet in him was born, a
tantalizing birthplace lost in obscurity, with doors
opening from the back on ulterior paths leading
away in the other direction, the direction of the
mirror. ' Have you ever,' he said, ' seen that door?
. . . its ruinous stone lintel, carved into lichenous
stone heads, stonily silent in the last thin sunlight,

hanging in peace unlatched. Heated, hunted, in
agony—in that cold, green-clad, shadowed porch is
haven and sanctuary.   But beyond—O God, beyond!'

That is the keynote of his work, and the goad
which whips him on to ever more tense and distilled self-expression; an artist consumed by his own
nerves, yet always emerging from the terror to a
sort of humour and appetite for life, finding an
equipoise in his own pain, and a fecundity from
the contradiction which has torn his life.

ROBERT FROST: A PROPHET IN HIS OWN COUNTRY

Some twenty-five miles from London stands a beech-tree. It is a vast creature, with its man-flesh twisted and gnarled into all sorts of gargoyle-like shapes. It has a personality; powerful, assertive, yet secretive. Its huge back, if a tree can be said to have a back, is turned to the road, and it looks down along the bottom of the southward-sloping wood of which it is the outpost. It has a political purpose, for it marks the boundary between Surrey and Kent.

But it has a greater history than that. Round its gouty roots winds a footpath, leading from the road under the wood and along the open country to the left. This old giant is a sort of grumpy concierge guarding the privileges of that footpath. Most people would pass it by. But a few, with associations and a reverence for the past, would stop, and raise a hat, before passing on down the road to the gate where they will meet a view of forty miles across and along the Weald.

For that path leads to a house called The Cerne. Some people, reading this article and coming to this name, will at once know what I am leading to.

They will know that house as Mohammedans know Mecca. It was the home of Edward Garnett, his wife Constance, and his son David. Two of them are still living, and famous figures in contemporary literature, so I cannot say more about them, except to point out that David Garnett has written a marvellous semi-fiction about that house and its garden hanging under the shadow of the hill and the wood. He is an infrequent writer; but he is possessed of that distillation of personality which we call genius.

It is a fitting thing that he should be the son of Edward Garnett, the man who built The Cerne and made it a place of pilgrimage for writers and aspirants over a period of more than thirty years. During that time the little footpath leading through the wood was trodden by many feet destined later to tread the narrower path of fame. And it was Edward Garnett who guided them from the first path to the second. And all of them must have passed the old beech-tree. (If you go there now, you won't find it, for a blast of lightning struck it and consumed it soon after Edward Garnett's death. That, too, seems appropriate.) Some of the survivors of that traffic should be approached, and asked to make a contribution towards an anthology commemorating The Cerne. Joseph Conrad, Stephen Crane, Ford Madox Ford,

W. H. Hudson, Henry Brian Binns, E. V. Lucas,
Edward Thomas, John Galsworthy would not be
able to respond. But there are a few survivors still;
amongst them, W. H. Davies, de la Mare, and
Robert Frost.

I have already written here about two of those
survivors. I want now to say something about
Robert Frost and his work. I will begin by saying
that I am tempted to look upon him as a major
poet. A major poet is one who brings into a language and its poetry a new element of thought and
experience, and a new twist of phraseology. He
puts a thumb-mark upon his verse. Just as you
recognize immediately a house by Adam, or a
sonata by Beethoven, so you recognize a poem by
a major poet. It doesn't need to be signed. You
can tell by the way it walks who it is. You can
recognize Robert Frost's poetry in that way.

But Edward Garnett was the first thus to recognize
it. Robert Frost came as a young man in the early
years of the present century to Europe. He left
his home in New England, a ' plain New Hampshire
farmer ' as he describes himself, a prophet in his
own country; ignored and unknown. Perhaps pique
and despair drove him to this excursion, though
I cannot imagine so serene a spirit being so

self-indulgent.   Whatever the origin of that impulse,
it proved to be one of those calls of pre-destiny which
seem to summon all creative men.

He came to England, was drawn into the magnetic
circle of Edward Garnett, and did not leave it until
he returned to America soon after the outbreak of
the last war (which I heard referred to the other day,
by a young one-pip lieutenant, as ' that insignificant
war '). He returned to find himself famous in his
native land. That is no small achievement. It is
reminiscent, in a lighter vein, of the career of Dante,
who wandered in exile round the periphery of
Florence while his reputation steadily grew in that
forbidden birthplace. Certainly Frost's reputation
was a reflection from that which had already been
made in England; and made by the championing of
Edward Garnett. For it seems that a poet needs an
influential advocate as well as a sound achievement
of good work, before he is recognized.

The advocacy was particularly valuable to this
poet, because his work is of a nature to grow
slowly, and to win adherents slowly. He had
something new to say, or rather to sing: and the
scales on which he made his music were oddly
subtle. He composed in quarter-tones, suiting his
music to his moods and his ideas, experiences of

microscopic graduation that needed a new technique to measure them. The influence was new to English poetry, and it is still felt. One aspect of it, for example, affects the verse of our contemporary Andrew Young, a writer whose delicacy of vision and expression is tributary to the same quality in the poetry of Robert Frost.

What is this new element which Frost has brought? It is difficult to define, because it is a quality of the man, of his whole personality and outlook on life. It is also something which is local, belonging to the people, the stock from which he springs. It is a characteristic of New England Puritanism, and its source may thus be traced back a long way until we find it originating in the Home Country, amongst the Quakers and Wesleyans of the eighteenth century. It is a complicated element (if that is not a contradiction in terms). It is a combination of quietism, piety with its underlying enthusiasm, suspicion of this world and especially of the world of man, self-restraint with its ever - imminent abandonment, humility with its threat of arrogance. There is a negativeness about these forces. They have a sort of dove-grey colour, like the cloak of a Quakeress. But how restful that colour is, how tender, how evocative of the latent beauty of all other hues with which it comes into contact! They represent a whole period of English history. It is that period which included the break away of the American branch, and established a community in New England more emphatic of the same power than the trunk from which it sprang.

Many sociologists to-day believe that this quality of quietism, of exerting authority by means of understatement, is doomed to extinction beneath the flood of barbaric noise brought in by the machine, the radio, and the dictator. I don't believe it. The United States, which is supposed to be the pioneer of latter-day hustle and go-getting, is saturated in this spirit of allusiveness, of understatement, of quiet emphasis. Examine the pages of the New Yorker, that hard-boiled humorous journal, and you will find that its technique has much in common with that which Robert Frost accentuated in English poetry thirty-five years ago. It is a native technique; that of the laconic Yankee. And it originated in England, latent from the days of Chaucer, recognized and organized from the days of great Protestant writers at the end of the seventeenth century. Robert Frost is thus a spokesman of his own people. He is probably a more representative American than Walt Whitman. That is why his fame has not been a

temporary one.   His work needed only to be pointed
out to the self-distrustful Americans, and they at
once recognized it as something near home, something expressing their own habits, their own point
of view, their own reaction to the society which
they were still building, and the wild nature which
they were still only beginning to subdue and to
appreciate.

We all need to get things outside ourselves before
we can see them and appreciate them.   Robert Frost
thus did his people as well as himself a service by
leaving home and settling for a decade in Europe.
Further, the scenery and the folk of England stirred
something ancestral in him, waking his instincts to
a fuller consciousness.   He strengthened those instincts by means of a fine detachment, which
enabled him to objectify the material from which
his verse was made, and to give the result a universality without spoiling its local flavour.   As he says:

> Anything I can say about New Hampshire
> Will serve almost as well about Vermont,

and equally as well about old Hampshire in England
and the most conservative inhabitant thereof.   Will
not that native of the Old World recognize, for
example, the poet's expression in the following lyric
of that perennial grudge which we all feel against

the summer because of what it has snatched from spring?

> These pools that, though in forests, still reflect
> The total sky almost without defect,
> And like the flowers beside them, chill and shiver,
> Will like the flowers beside them soon be gone,
> And yet not out by any brook or river,
> But up by roots to bring dark foliage on.
> The trees that have it in their pent-up buds
> To darken nature and be summer woods—
> Let them think twice before they use their powers
> To blot out and drink up and sweep away
> These flowery waters and these watery flowers
> From snow that melted only yesterday.

That may be only a fanciful piece, but it is characteristic of the man in his maturity, with his moods given a universal value and simplicity.

The simplicity is the quality which most marks him. He has practised it until he can make it convey the most subtle ideas and emotions. Such a practice should be the main preoccupation of a poet. It is the one which made Wordsworth great. When he was rhetorical and ornamental he was a tasteless bore. Frost is even more single than Wordsworth in this pursuit of simplicity. It is another aspect of his inherited puritanism; and the other outstanding feature of his work, its marvellous utilization of the laconic, is only another develop-

ment of this same quality. And the discipline necessary for the constant refining down of a poetic nature
to this purpose has added something else to that
nature; a gift of humour; a humour wry, dry, sharp,
but an eager participant in the process of unifying a
personality.

That personality I have always found very much
to my liking. There is no other poet to whom he
can be compared. Even his English disciple Edward
Thomas, to whom I shall refer again in a moment,
is different. Frost seems, for one thing, always to
choose the disappearances of human life and of wild
nature as symbols to fit his moods. His is the genius
of shyness, and its abbreviated gestures may be over-
looked by the reader who expects to find the fine
exaggerations so common to poetry. You have to
watch for the flicker of an eyelid, and even then it
may not come. That failure would be intentional,
and you would discover afterwards the meaning of
it, and chuckle to yourself with satisfaction, and a
deep gratitude toward that deliberately half-articu-
lated wisdom. As for this poet's music, that too
has an intentional flatness and whimsicality, like the
whirr of the nightjar, that sound which can make
the common, neglected spots become magical with
a sort of drab expectancy.

It is often useful, but probably restrictive, to quote from a poet passages which seem to sum up his character and his method. Every original character has such moments of self-betrayal. Here are two such revealing passages.

> By June our brook's run out of song and speed.
> Sought for much after that, it will be found
> Either to have gone groping underground
> (And taken with it all the Hyla breed
> That shouted in the mist a month ago,
> Like ghosts of sleigh-bells in a ghost of snow)—
> Or flourished and come up in jewel-weed,
> Weak foliage that is blown upon a bent
> Even against the way its waters went.
> Its bed is left a faded paper sheet
> Of dead leaves stuck together by the heat—
> A brook to none but who remember long.
> This as it will be seen is other far
> Than with brooks taken otherwhere in song.
> We love the things we love for what they are.

This brook that just dries up and is lost, is typical of the people, places, and moods that attract this poet; something gone, but still here: something that perhaps may never have been, yet probably must have been. These powerful and life-veering intangibilities, and the clouds of beauty trailing after them, constitute the interests of Frost's life. Yet with these quaint interests runs a shrewd sense of

Robert Frost

reality; a sly, farmer-like wisdom, thrown out in asides and hints, full of knowing-kindness and ancient malice. Shrunken, crabbed human nature, toughened by contact with earth, is good enough for Mr Frost, and he sings of it in a strange, yet half-familiar strain:

> a singer every one has heard,
> Loud, a midsummer and a midwood bird,
> Who makes the solid tree-trunks sound again.
> He says that leaves are old and that for flowers
> Midsummer is to spring as one to ten.
> He says the early petal-fall is past
> When pear and cherry bloom went down in
>   showers
> On sunny days a moment overcast;
> And comes that other fall we name the fall.
> He says the highway dust is over all.
> The bird would cease and be as other birds
> But that he knows in singing not to sing.
> The question that he frames in all but words
> Is what to make of a diminished thing.

Those last three lines are an explanation of this poet's technique, that seeks out awkwardnesses and makes music from them; a queer sort of music, like that of a hidden waterfall in a wood, which strikes into the deeps of a man's nature.

You see, too, the laughter which is lurking in this poet's work. It is a serious laughter, folded over

D

tenderness and love, ringing through his poems,
toning down the high lights, lifting up the shadows,
and intensifying that laconic monotone, at first
strange to the ear, which becomes dearer and more
entrancing by familiarity. And with this laughter,
there trembles a note of passion, and deep understanding of the conflict of mind with heart, of man
with woman, of humanity with the forces of life
and death. This laughter is a savour through all
his work, sometimes laconic and satirical, thrown
in at the last with a sort of over-shoulder word,
sometimes breaking through even the lyrical mood
(one traditionally lacking in humour).

> The rain to the wind said
> ' You push and I 'll pelt.'
> They so smote the garden bed
> That the flowers actually knelt,
> And lay lodged—though not dead.
> I know how the flowers felt.

Laughter denotes detachment, and detachment denotes dramatic sense. Frost has that sense, and he
uses it as Browning did in a collection of narrative
poems, each of which deals with a tense situation
that he solves with humour, but sardonic humour
that delights in revealing the subtlety of false endings, inconclusive endings, irrelevancies; devices

which real life abounds in, but literature is shy of.
But Frost loves such implicit criticism of human
and natural affairs.   Gathering up dead leaves in his
autumn garden, he comments that they are

> Next to nothing for use.
> But a crop is a crop,
> And who's to say where
> The harvest shall stop?

That is his philosophy.   Reject nothing; but mini-
mize it, in order to see it more roundly, and to locate
it in its place in the chain of endless eventuality.   So
though his work is so quiet, it is not static.   He
pretends to step aside, as observer, from the universal mobility.   But he also makes poetry out of
that pretence.   Indeed, it is the source of his laughter.

Such is the poet who came to England, unknown,
and showed his work to Edward Garnett nearly
forty years ago.   Garnett at once realized the quality
of it, and sponsored it.   He introduced Frost to
other writers, amongst them a sensitive young critic
and country-writer, Edward Thomas, at that time a
man almost broken by overwork.   The friendship
gave new life to Thomas.   Under the stimulus of
Frost's personality, he began to write verse, and
continued to do so until he was killed on Vimy
Ridge.   The body of poetry Thomas has left is

unique. It obviously owes something to the larger
voice of Robert Frost, but it has its personal rhythm,
and time is therefore treating it kindly.

I like to think of these two men meeting at The
Cerne, and of the regeneration of an exhausted spirit
taking place, perhaps, during a stroll through the
wood out to the road. The American poet and the
English would have stood for a few moments under
that giant beech-tree where the path runs along the
county border; and Thomas would have been in-
spired by the other man's deep well of humility

> If, as they say, some dust thrown in my eyes
> Will keep my talk from getting overwise,
> I 'm not the one for putting off the proof.
> Let it be overwhelming, off a roof
> And round a corner, blizzard snow for dust,
> And blind me to a standstill if it must.

But it was Thomas who was to be handled thus.
At least, he was the first. I suspect that Robert
Frost is still awaiting that medicine. And that is
why he remains alert, and still a poet with sudden
and beautiful things to say.

Fifty years ago, when W. B. Yeats was a young man of twenty-three, he wrote the following words in the course of a review of a book of verse long since forgotten. 'When a literature is old it grows so indirect and complex that it is only a possession for the few: to read it well is a difficult pursuit, like playing the fiddle; for it one needs especial training.'

English literature is certainly at the stage described by that far-seeing young poet. And in its latter half-century it has aged rapidly, so that at present, while the storm rages, all it can do is to sit huddled in a corner under the chimney, with a glass of warming oblivion by its side. This allegory, at least, may be used of our poetry to-day. The small group of poets who did show signs of getting into touch with the general reading public—and it did little more than that—has been silenced by the war. But it is still too soon to dogmatize about that.

With the young men silent, and Yeats dead, there is an emptiness, a silence. How and when will it be broken? We don't know. We can only look back; listen back with memory's ear. And what recurs to us most clearly, almost overwhelmingly, is the giant figure of Yeats. It is Yeats as an old man, savage in his struggle with Time, beating back the tide with great gestures of vituperation, his white hair blowing in the wind, one eye only visible, the other blacked out with an opaque lens; the green stone of his signet ring flashing as he lifts his hand and clenches it against the enemy.

It is a tragic picture, of a man discontented with his achievement, a man fighting more fiercely at the end than at the beginning of his life, a man with little fundamental pleasure in his fame. But it is also a triumphant picture, as we see the white-haired poet, sick and maimed, convulsed still with the fire of creative effort, straining still to the necessary labour of capturing the real phrase of poetry, and not a latter-day literary simulacrum of it.

It is a recurring mystery, this of the swan-song. We note how frequently in the lives of poets there is a period of great productivity in youth, a lull during the years of maturity, and then another lyrical burst in old age. It is like the history of a summer day. Up comes the sun, with a slant fire throwing a wild illumination upon the most ordinary of things; raising mists and veils, patching colours upon the drab, and shadow-patterns beyond the flattest objects. Then comes midday, with a vertical sun. Light pours over everything alike; flattens all things out, dries all things up. The very brightness of noon seems to concentrate into a kind of blue darkness, oppressive, ominous. No bird sings. But towards evening a breeze springs up, blows perfumes about, turns leaves to catch the oblique light. Birds break into song deeper, more lucid and prophetic than that of dawn. And the sun goes down in splendour, a magnificent solitary with no rival in the sky.

We have just witnessed such a sunset in the passing of Yeats. Was that solitariness an illusion put upon us by his old age? I do not think so. At the same time as he wrote those words about an ancient literature, he said also that 'the modern author, if he be a man of genius, is a solitary; he does not know the ever-changing public well enough to be their servant. He cannot learn their convention; they must learn his. All that is greatest in modern literature is soliloquy, or, at most, words addressed to a few friends.' It is true of his own career, for in spite of his success, and the early appreciation ' of a few friends,' his public was never big enough to bring him more than two hundred pounds a year until he was past fifty years of age.

I bring in this reference to money because what people want they will pay for. The Victorians wanted Tennyson's poems so much that publishers were glad to pay him a retaining fee of seven thousand a year on seven-year contracts! The comparison is nicely ironic. Dr Johnson would have appreciated it, and drawn from it a conclusion about the aesthetic value of the two poets' work. It also appears to offer some confirmation of Yeats's argument about ' the modern author, if he be a man of genius.'

So Yeats worked, unremunerated, through the heyday of his life, producing the long, swinging lyrics of his youth, and the plays about Irish heroes and demigods. But a time came, in the teens and twenties of the present century, when even the few grew weary of the Celtic twilight. Yeats's work began to pall. Derisive legends grew up round his name. He was called a poseur. A cruel critic wrote about the fur-lined overcoat with which he returned to Ireland after a successful lecture tour in America. Other critics, more deadly, attacked him because of his dallyings with Madame Blavatsky, his pseudo-orientalism, his dippings into esoterics and occultism. There were quarrels at the Abbey Theatre, and boycottings in Bloomsbury.

It was the noonday darkness. What was he really

doing during this time? What was the significance
of the obscure studies? And were they indeed
sufficiently disinterested to be called studies? I
believe that one ought to look somewhat askance
upon a poet's studies. He never studies for the sake
of the subject, as a scholar should. He has an
ulterior motive. Yeats says of himself: 'I remember
some old man, a stranger to me, saying, "I have
watched you for the past half-hour and you have
neither made a note nor read a word." I am
certain that everybody outside my own little circle
who knew anything about me thought as did that
cross old man, for I was arrogant, indolent, excitable.'

It was the excitement of the bee, that pryer into
rich volumes, who is always hard at work honeying
his own hive. That was one reason for Yeats's studies
in the occult. Another was that described by a critic
recently, who said that 'Yeats sensed that in the study
of the occult, man might surprise the secret that would
free him from the despotism of unhappiness.'

The search led the poet into many dark places,
and it threw strange obscurations across his poetry
when he began to sing again. Much discussion has
gone on among the critics about this element in his
verse. They called it a new element, and some
blamed his studies for it. Others, more reverent,

proceeded to exegesis, timidly believing that where there is obscurity there must be virtue. One volume in particular, The Tower, published in 1928, came with such force of intellectual novelty that critics and public together were surprised into a new attention to the poet whom they had begun to take for granted. The old gods of Ireland were still to be found in this book; but they had thrown off their fancy dress, their starry brooches and scabbards. They were now elemental monsters of the naked mind, too near and too active to be merely symbols of the poet's agony. They stood about him like a crowd of living and angry men, hiding him for the time being. He was certainly lost in the figures which he had conjured: He had caught himself up in the machinery of living, and had to summon these literary giants out of his past to extricate him.

> A man in his own secret meditation
> Is lost amid the labyrinth that he has made
> In art or politics;
> Some platonist affirms that in the station
> Where we should cast off body and trade
> The ancient habit sticks,
> And that if our works could
> But vanish with our breath
> That were a lucky death,
> For triumph can but mar our solitude.

Still that harping on solitude. And what makes a man a solitary? It is because he has a secret which he wishes to preserve. Yeats's secret was the knowledge that the way he made his poetry was not the way the critics thought he made it. He took a malicious delight in fostering this misbelief. He heard the loud chatter of his disciples dissertating upon his enormous scholarship, his infinite pains. He encouraged the legend about the making of one quatrain occupying a whole morning of exhausting labour. The process is recognizable. Browning had already patented it. He, too, made a cult of his old age and its wisdom and erudition, delighting to tease the Browning Society with posers in verse. In consequence, much of his later work is now unreadable. But at the very end his genius—another word for simplicity and native innocence—broke through this web of sophistication and vanity and malice, and in *Asolando* he sang as lucidly as ever he had done in his youth.

Yeats never sank quite so deeply into self-obscurantism. Even in his most tangled work, in his despair and fear at the approach of old age, the smoke screen of intellectual snobbery which he threw round himself was never thick enough to hide the figure at the core. In the book *The Tower* we

find again and again flashes of a severe simplicity
which really do utilize all that mental stuff, and
make it terrible with the fierce direction of the poet.
Such moments were already prophetic. They showed
him preoccupied not only with his own doom, but
with the doom of European civilization. Indeed, that
latter premonition was with him all his life. He
was always a savage critic of the machine and its
vulgarizing and brutalizing influence. No artist has
ever so much hated mass production, the technique
by which the machine threatens to destroy the flower
of human nature. To-day, we see it at work, with
thousands of German tanks treading over Europe,
and the theories of the Nazi shouting from a box
in every household in the Old World and the New.

In his youth he spoke of these things: 'The struggle
of labour and capital, of mysticism and science, and
many another contest now but dimly foreshadowed,
will more and more absorb or deafen into silence all
such cloistered lives—the products of periods of rest
between two worlds, " one dead, one powerless to
be born." ' We are now standing at that deathbed.
And to-morrow we shall have to turn, those of us
who remain, and work as midwives at the 'powerless
birth' which Yeats foresaw fifty years ago. The
lament which runs through all his life-work, the

source of its anger and sorrow, are to be found in this vision, which never left him.

> In pity for man's darkening thought
> He walked that room and issued thence
> In Galilean turbulence;
> The Babylonian Starlight brougnt
> A fabulous, formless darkness in;
> Odour of blood when Christ was slain
> Made Plato's tolerance in vain
> And vain the Doric discipline.

Those last three lines, from the Tower volume, have a dreadful directness in their comment on what is happening in Europe to-day. They summarize the historical significance of the whole struggle; the attack on Christianity, on the individual soul, on gracious thought and instinct, on the free order of reason. Yeats's weakening physical force was already acting upon his pride, dissolving it away and bringing to the surface a harder self.

> Bodily decrepitude is wisdom; young
> We loved each other and were ignorant.

After The Tower came The Winding Stair, in which he threw aside all camouflage of intellectualism, and went straight back to reminiscence of his whole life as an artist. But the glancing backward was still

done with a purpose, which was to warn the present
generation of the coming catastrophe.

> We were the last romantics—chose for theme
> Traditional sanctity and loveliness;
> Whatever's written in what poets name
> The book of the people; whatever most can bless
> The mind of man or elevate a rhyme;
> But all is changed, that high horse riderless,
> Though mounted in that saddle Homer rode
> Where the swan drifts upon a darkening flood.

He sees it coming closer and closer, and it fills
him with the conviction that he must do something active, beyond that making of poetry.

> Although the summer sunlight gild
> Cloudy leafage of the sky,
> Or wintry moonlight sink the field
> In storm-scattered intricacy,
> I cannot look thereon,
> Responsibility so weighs me down.

We see him after this active in politics, speaking
and commanding attention in the Irish Senate. And
we watch him withdrawing in disgust from the
commerce of it. It was at this time that I saw something of him, and had many talks with him in
London. On one occasion he said something which
showed me into the secret that made his solitude,
and which makes the solitude of all true poets

'The trouble with the young English poets of to-
day,' he said, 'is that they are too conscientious.
They don't trust enough to luck.' It looks a simple
saying. But it contains the unjust truth about the
art of poetry. It reveals how unfair is the compact
between the poet and his Daemon; the tricks they
get up to between them. It shows why the poet
is so shy of the erudite, and why he pours scorn on
'remote ineffectual dons.' It shows too why poets
are crazy creatures, consumed with worry about
where the next word is coming from, agonizing
lest they may have said their last magic phrase, dreading
lest their elusive partner may have let them down.   It
explains, too, Yeats's lifelong devotion to William
Blake, and his wilful pleasure in the Prophetic
Books, those poetic eloquences which have not quite
come off. Yeats at last realized the blindness of
man, the endowment of chance, the dependence
upon something which he is never able to command,
the life of rule of thumb, of trial and error, a poet
living like a gardener or a sailor, at the mercy of the
elements.

> A living man is blind and drinks his drop.
> What matter if the ditches are impure?
> What matter if I live it all once more?
> Endure that toil of growing up;

The ignominy of boyhood; the distress
Of boyhood changing into man;
The unfinished man and his pain
Brought face to face with his own clumsiness.

I am content to follow to its source
Every event in action or in thought;
Measure the lot; forgive myself the lot;
When such as I cast out remorse
So great a sweetness flows into the breast
We must laugh and we must sing,
We are blest by everything,
Everything we look upon is blest.

How dangerous it all is; and how exhilarating.
The perfumed winds of youth revive, the divine
waywardness seizes upon the spirit, making disil-
lusion itself a surprise and a delight. It is a state of
chance and caprice which is native to Yeats. He had
been so all his life, and all the affectations and worldly
poses as savant, cult-leader, deliberating theorist,
were never able to overlay the innocent and the
wilful creature, the poet. Did he ever trouble even
to be consistent in his attitude to the world? Only
a few years ago, in his preface to the Oxford Book of
Modern Verse, he left out war poems, arguing that
'passive suffering is not a theme for poetry.' A
storm of protest blew round him. But he did not
reply. He had probably forgotten what he had said.

Now, in his posthumous volume of *Last Poems, Last Plays*, he says:

> You that Mitchel's prayer have heard,
> ' Send war in our time, O Lord,'
> Know that when all words are said
> And a man is fighting mad,
> Something drops from eyes long blind,
> He completes his partial mind,
> For an instant stands at ease,
> Laughs aloud, his heart at peace.
> Even the wisest man grows tense
> With some sort of violence
> Before he can accomplish fate,
> Know his work or choose his mate.

This last volume is astonishing in its poetic rich-
ness. Every poem in it is stark and memorable.
He asks: 'Why should not old men be mad?' Why
not, indeed, if their madness produce such music as
this? And what music is it? It is the music which
has been native in him since he began to sing more
than fifty years ago; a music wayward, dangerous,
always hovering upon uncertainty, springing like a
child's delights out of small but concrete things.

> Those masterful images because complete
> Grew in pure mind, but out of what began?
> A mound of refuse or the sweepings of a street,
> Old kettles, old bottles, and a broken can,

E

Old iron, old bones, old rags, that raving slut
Who keeps the till.   Now that my ladder's gone,
I must lie down where all the ladders start,
In the foul rag-and-bone shop of the heart.

That is a fitting last word from a man whose whole
life has been spent in a passionate curiosity, the
curiosity which children know and lose, and which
poets know and keep.

W. B. Yeats

EDMUND BLUNDEN: AGONIST

During the last quarter of a century, the poetic generations have become swift and short. I remember hearing an elder poet—who in spite of his fame hates to be mentioned in print by his friends—say that to-day a generation of poets lasts for five years, and that on its heels another treads so close that it acquires a stiff neck from looking back in dread.

There is much truth in that humour. A poet does not arrive now: he only rests on a ledge, while those down below pot at him with the guns of derisive envy. See how Hardy, Housman, and the picturesque Rupert Brooke have been treated by our younger critics. They don't believe in ' live and let live.' Such a policy is too laisser-faire for them, smacking of the old liberalism which they so rabidly despise. Think, too, of their contempt for the group they call the Georgians, a classification which they use to include all poets between the ages of sixty-five and forty-five, irrespective of their work, and of the past vicissitudes which it encountered while these young savagers were still in the nursery.

I say, irrespective of their work; and I think

particularly of the poetry of Edmund Blunden. How curiously it has suffered. At the beginning, when in the early twenties he sprang suddenly into notice with poems in Massingham's *Nation* and Squire's *London Mercury*, it was readily agreed amongst the monitors of that time that here was a new voice of real importance, one which would make old tradition blossom again like the rose. Following this recognition, the young poet wrote a war-book in somewhat self-conscious prose, which carried him to a more general fame amongst the public not interested in poetry. After that, he retired into the monastery of Merton College, and has since been heard of only in the cruel headnotes of the young derisionists. They have sneered at his ' nature ' poetry, as they call it; and they have said more sinister things about reactionary political tendencies in the author of it. I have not heard a word of praise amongst them. I have not met a single disciple.

How very strange that is; for Blunden has never, in his literary career, said or done anything—as did the late Humbert Wolfe—to arouse antagonism. Wolfe, when at the height of his success, was realist enough to be frightened by it, and acted in public with a certain amount of affected flamboyance and audacity. He reached up and patted giants on the

head—Hardy, for example. This so enraged a contemporary that he wrote a book of parodies which
snuffed Wolfe out like a candle. It was unfair, for
Wolfe was fundamentally a generous soul, both in
life and literature, and his audacity was more fun
than anything else.

But Blunden has never indulged in such indiscre-
tions. I doubt if he even knows of the existence of
work by his contemporaries. His literary interests
stopped short with the death of Charles Lamb. After
that, for him, it is darkness, except for the illumination of his own candle, past which he peers with
beady eyes, like a startled mouse looking for the
cat. But with this self-absorption, both in life and
letters, one would think that Blunden could attract
no enmities or envies. One would think that the
younger poets would know where they were with
him; they would know that he had never heard of
them, nor wanted to, and was content to let them
take the limelight, and the whole of the political
platform—which was what they seemed mostly to
want. In spite of this, however, they have savaged
him. And in spite of them, he is still working, as
we see from his new collection of poems covering
the period 1930–40. This collection carries on from
the earlier one covering the period 1914–30. In

the two we have practically the whole of his output
in verse, and from them we can make a general
survey of its development.

First, let us take the world which appeared before
the flood overwhelmed him; that flood which shook
all his contemporaries. Not one escaped. Now
that the flood is subsiding after the war has knocked
the bottom out of the School of College Communism,
and sent its leader flying to America, we see that not
even Mr Eliot has escaped the inundation. His
famous dust-bin lies overturned in the silt. And
in that position it appears to be past further use,
especially at a time when the civilization which
Mr Eliot derided is throwing itself out of its own
door on to its own rubbish heap.

But these are temporary matters. ' Civilizations
break and bend '; but we are concerned at the moment
with their distillation, their permanent residue—
poetry. After the hurricane, it comes like a calm
rain, which fecundates the torn world once more.
Blunden has been aware of the whole process, and
refers to it thus:

> So this still rain beguiled my mood and verse,
> But I awake; I dreamed; what worth is his
> Who fashions thus a selfish universe,
> And weaves dead leaves with living tragedies?

While the strong world goes forth in symphonies
Of action, passion, science and resource,
Where shall faint music and far similes
Befriend it? has this stealing shower a force?
And yet I fancy sometimes there is pain
That still requires this shy and dream-like rain.

Old-fashioned, isn't it? And this is the later man speaking, in a poem from the 1930–40 volume. But let it penetrate; let it get past the mind, the mood, the present-day preoccupation, and see if it waters the soul, that internal self which is deeper than our consciousness and our experience.

This quotation suggests that the poet is not unaware of the conditions, the problems, the literary conflicts and fashions, which have contributed to his seeming eclipse. That awareness was alive in him when he wrote the preface to his volume in 1930. 'The titles and contents of my books The Waggoner and The Shepherd have, I apprehend, done me a slight injustice; that is, they have labelled me among poets of the time as a useful rustic, or perhaps not so useful—one of the class whom the song describes:

I sits with my feet in a brook;
   If any one asks me for why,
I hits him a whack with my crook—
   "It's Sentiment kills me," says I.

Great as is the power of country life over me, and
of that stately march of the seasons above, around,
below it, yet I have always suspected myself of some
inclination to explore other subjects.' Of one of
those subjects, the malevolence of Time, I will speak
in a moment, after I have discussed the technique
which he so quickly perfected during his devotion
to the poet John Clare. How can I best describe
the peculiar effect of that technique? He does not
break the poetic conventions with it, although in
metre his experiments are varied enough. It is an
instrument so precise to the requirements of his
nature that I find I cannot discuss it without a simul-
taneous consideration of the element in his work
which I proposed to discuss later. That element is
Time. It is his adversary as it was Thomas Hardy's,
and it has to be propitiated, and finally absorbed
into his acceptance of the scheme of things. This
conflict with Time plays such an enormous part in
his poetry because his experiences during the last
war accentuated, to the point of madness, the possibilities of chance and change which can be brought
about by the mere passage of moments. This tragic
sense of the mutability of things pervades his work,
and it stains his phrases and images so emphatically,
that no adverse critic could accuse his verse of being

colourless, or lacking in a personal thumb-mark.
Here is something far more desperate than all the
political and social injustices with which his de-
tractors have filled their verse, and which they have
said should be a poet's main interest. Their metro-
politan fervours sound, to my ear, mechanical after
the rush and roar of time's passage as Mr Blunden
hears it. Old Heracleitus, the philosopher who believed that the universe was made from the single
element of Fire, would say that this rush and roar
are the inevitable movement of combustion; the
lovely shapes, situations, forms, loves, and thoughts
burning out from their complicated and separate
beauty down into the ashes of unified oblivion and
peace. That is a conception which haunts many
minds. It underlies the variety of Blunden's interests, and gives a quality of anxiety to that quick,
prying nervousness with which he ferrets out the
joy of the world. It conditions all his acceptances
of the appearance of things, and hedges them about
with terror. He can trust nothing, not even the
lovely manifestations of nature towards which he
turns for healing of his war-wounded spirit. See,
for instance, how he looks on at a party of skaters
at midnight.

The hop-poles stand in cones,
The icy pond lurks under,
The hop-poles steeple to the thrones
Of stars, sound gulfs of wonder;
But not the tallest there, 'tis said,
Could fathom to this pond's black bed.

Then is not death at watch
Within those secret waters?
What wants he but to catch
Earth's heedless sons and daughters?
With but a crystal parapet
Between, he has his engines set.

Then on, blood shouts, on, on,
Twirl, wheel and whip above him,
Dance on this ball-floor thin and wan,
Use him as though you love him;
Court him, elude him, reel and pass,
And let him hate you through the glass.

Here, surely, is no bucolic escapist. Here is a
poet who finds in the countryside as bitter a waste
land as Mr Eliot found in the back streets of the
town. Instead of the old sardine tins and the stray
cats round the dustbins, he chooses thistles for symbols
of the sardonic:

Thistles, most, jump from the marl,
Baring teeth in sudden snarl.
Perhaps when Magog was a child

They grew in gardens, lilies wild;
Injured here, they nurse their grievance;
Briars and nettles nod connivance.

Is it not the same conflict; very much contemporary? With him, its effect is most extraordinary. While in mind and apprehension he seems always to be on thorns, always to be half-exhausted in an effort to touch everything that nature manifests, yet for the expressing of his experiences during this quest he has evolved a poetry which is as calm and slow-moving as any in the language. Like Keats', his spirit is fevered with the greed for 'beauty and truth,' and like Keats', his verse is loaded, verbally architectured, static. Again and again he gets deliberate effects by the use of double accents, or spondees.

The cuckoo with a strong flute,
The orchard with a mild sigh,
Bird and blossom so salute
The rainbow sky.

The brown herd in the green shade,
The parson in his lawn chair,
Poor and gentry both evade
The furnace air.

The moon-inveigled mushroom,
The crocus with her frail horn,
Gaze in dumb dread through the gloom
Of late moist morn.

The dead leaf on the highlands,
The old tramp on the mill drove,
Each whirls on nor understands
God's freezing love.

It is as though he is conscious of his fears, and by
an effort of will tries to slow himself, to calm down
his scared imagination to an accordance with the
steady, loaded measures of his verse.   But an artist's
prevailing mood will always make itself felt in his
technique, if only in a negative way.   You will find
in Blunden's rich lines a careful supply of old-
fashioned words, many of them so archaic that
Robert Bridges took the trouble to write a pamphlet
about them.   We find his early poems, those written
up to 1930, decorated with such words as ' whirry,'
' clote,' ' elmen,' ' kerchered.'   This practice reflects
his effort to capture, before they have vanished, the
myriad details of the setting where he lived his
childhood before the war changed both him and
the place where his ancestors dwelled and accumu-
lated through century after century a tradition of
local interest, but universal significance.

Unrecorded, unrenowned,
Men from whom my ways begin,
Here I know you by your ground

> But I know you not within—
> There is silence, there survives
> Not a moment of your lives.

There is that time element again, ever eluding
him. He ransacks that past, watching with agony
the decaying of it as each familiar thing ' whirls on
nor understands God's freezing love.' As we read,
we begin to perceive that strain of madness in the
work, kindled by frenzy. To this almost abnormal
sensibility, the war came only as a fiendish accen-
tuation of the destructive process, making the poet
cling with even greater conservative fears to the
past. Is that what the young moderns object to in
him? Are they embarrassed as he pries about closer
and closer among 'the tiny circumstances of peace'
and mourns, with heart-breaking pathos, their
mutilation and ruin? In his gesture of defiance he
almost stands as the declared enemy of change,
progress, experiment, or any other force that erases
before it builds. And that is blasphemy to-day.

I should not give a true picture of Blunden's work,
however, if I left it on a note of agony, especially
when I consider the general mood of his volume
covering the last ten years, in which he emphasizes
again and again that ' there's a grace in monotony,'
and revels in the delights of a quietism shared with

a companion whose influence has brought some effective antidote to the poison of time and the shattering experiences of the last war. Apart from this influence, a personal one which the critic cannot yet discuss, is the fact that Blunden has always valued so passionately the 'tiny circumstances' of the world, and found in them a joy so abundant that it overflows his heart and saturates every phrase which is making under his hands. He has a great gift of descriptive evocation, both of general and detailed scenes. He misses nothing. He picks out shy, odd things, the minutest happenings, the most shadowy of moods, and peers at them by the light of his robin-lantern curiosity. And what he discovers there is always related by him to the huge stock of scenes and deeds and moods stored in his mind, a *cache* of book treasures, the glories of other poets—except those of his own time—whose work is a part of our English scenery and atmosphere, and whose genius haunts our lanes and cottages, like swallows at nightfall.

In consequence, his ideas are always de-personalized by the time he has finished this subtle manipulation. He seems to hide his feeling behind his thought, and to deprecate, in almost an orgasm of shyness, the direct form of appeal to his reader. You approach

Edmund Blunden

him by the paths of scholarship, and unless you
know the road, with its literary signposts, you never
get near him or his meaning.   But having approached,
you discover a being of simple mood and impulse;
a creature eloquent with faith and that rare quality,
joy. Joy is the mainspring of his life and art. He
is always searching for it among the memories of
childhood, the only scene where he is assured of
no disappointment.

> Return; how stands that man enchanted
> Who, after seas and mountains crossed,
> Finds his old threshold, so long scanted,
> With not a rose or robin lost!
>
> The wise, from passion now retreating
> To the hamlets of the mind,
> In every glance have claimed the greeting
> Of spirits infinitely kind.

Finally, we may remark how, in that quest and
discovery of joy, his quick eye misses nothing.
The smallest insect in the pond, the drabbest weed in
the ditch, set him musing and creating a crowded
solitude.

> The magpies steering round from wood to wood,
> Tree-creeper flickering up the elm's green rind,
> Bold gnats that revel round my solitude
> And most this pleasant bee intent to find

The newborn joy, inveigle the rich mind
Long after darkness comes cold-lipped to one
Still listening to the bee, still basking in the sun.

To remove oneself from the particularities of his
patient vision and to look at his work as a whole is
like standing at some familiar point on the North
Downs, taking that wide southward view over the
Weald, on an eternal summer afternoon, when

Golden-age beckonings, lost pastoral things,
Fantastically near and far away,
Stretch in the sunny calm their blazoned wings.

The nearer slopes, hedges, fields; the clumps of
woodland, the oasts and spires, the middle-scene
uplands, and the distant line of whale-backs near the
coast, these are all both new and ancient to our eyes,
half-torturing us with a fullness of suggestion. We
have explored it all; but seen aloof it seems an
unapproachable land of longing. So it is with this
poetry by a Wealden man; a stretch of country of
the mind, in which one feels native, yet is ever
confronted with surprises that startle moments into
ecstasy outside the course of time.

V. SACKVILLE-WEST: A POET IN A TRADITION

While considering the work of Edmund Blunden, I remarked upon the pause in his reputation, due to the excitement of the last ten years, and the way in which it has overloaded the younger men's poetry with political and social obsession. Blunden's muse, with its preoccupations, was neglected. So, too, has been that of Victoria Sackville-West, another Kentish writer, another poet given to the exploration of solitude, to a private agony, and its assuagement in the delights of the soil. It will be interesting, therefore, to look at her work, especially as she also has published a volume of 'collected' poems, which suggests that she considers herself set in form and theme.

Another likeness between these two poets is their predilection toward an eighteenth-century manner of diction. But while with Mr Blunden it is due to his intense literary interests, with the other it is the outcome of something possibly more native, more inherent in her personality. It is difficult not to exaggerate in this matter, for merely in suggesting an eighteenth-century predilection I may give the impression that these poets are stiff, archaic. But

F   69

they are not. Both are passionate and immediate
in their work; more and more so as the reader grows
accustomed to their methods of self-expression.
The singularities of Miss Sackville-West's diction
reflect a correspondingly singular concentration of
interest, of emotion, upon a theme that is one of
the constants in English poetry, indeed in all poetry:
the relationship between man and the soil. Ranging
between extremes of realism and artificiality, poets
during the past two thousand years have put their
muse behind the plough and all that it represents.

Thus Miss Sackville-West is traditional, even old-
fashioned, both in matter and manner, and it may
be said at once that this reluctance frequently fetters
the spirit of her work, and encourages a personal
timidity through which it is the duty of an artist
to break. At its most repressive moments, it piles
up poetic phrases in her work, conventionalizes
emotions, and dodges behind literary echoes of form
and diction. Here is an example:

No lights are burning in the ivory tower
Like a tall lily in the moonlight risen;
No light, to-night, within the ivory prison.
No golden glow behind the blackened panes
Like golden anthers in a blackened flower;
The gates are looped, to-night, with hasps and chains.
Only the little virgin coldly smiling

V. Sackville-West

With carven finger raised to carven lip
In secrecy beneath the latticed moon
Preserves her secret, keeps her virgin watch
On silvered fields that to the silver heaven
Lie open as the restless summer sea
Crossed by one tall incautious sailing-ship,
Or love to lover generously given.

Indeed, no lights are burning in the ivory tower. But that is not the only tower which this poet inhabits. I should say that it is a place where she retreats during certain moods of weariness of mind, of defeatism, when confidence falls low, and her sense of purpose wavers. She is not often to be found there. Her more natural place is in a tower not of ivory, but of brick, a richly coloured house set in a richly coloured land, and furnished with a collection of treasures gathered by her as she has ranged over time, scholarship, and life. This tower, not pallid and circular, but eight-sided, represents at each angle an idiosyncrasy of the person within, whose vigour, sensuality, tenderness, imagination, passionate historical realism, compassion, practicalness, and common sense are graphed thereby. It is this poet, in this setting, with whom I am concerned in my effort to trace the course of my response to her work, and my conviction that this work has the quality of permanence.

Of course, there are poems coming from the ivory tower which have an air of authority about them. One of them I must quote, for it is as though a pagan Christina Rossetti had borrowed Alice Meynell's pen, and written something dangerous to them both.

Do not forget, my dear, that once we loved.
Remember only, free of stain or smutch,
That passion once went naked and ungloved,
And that your skin was startled by my touch.

And though the processes of mortal change
Delude you now to different belief,
Consider only that the heart 's a strange
Quick turn-coat, undeserving of your grief.

Forget,—regret,—should these two words be
    brothers?
If rhyme to rhyme be kith, so let them be!
Pass from my heart towards the heart of others;
But in your passing, half-remember me.

And from the dweller in the brick tower, with its eight angles of personality, come phrases, such as ' the tardy herd,' too indolently plucked from stock; while her strength, her close contact with fact, sometimes brings a stiffness, a humourless droop, such as Wordsworth displayed when he introduced his Mr Wilkinson to an awe-stricken world—but not awe-stricken in the sense that Wordsworth intended.

Now out of all this adverse criticism, the true poet, the author of The Land, Sissinghurst, and many other poems, emerges free. She is an artist who know herself, her faults, limitations, and the settlement of her interests. This last coincides with certain other settlements, and notably that of the decay, or change, of our rural civilization. There is thus a sort of preservative or recording value in her poem The Land, underlying its true poetic worth. The Land is a picture of certain aspects of an England which is vanishing; the England of a ripe and comely culture, which has been sung by Crabbe, Cowper, Thomson, Gray, Tennyson, Hardy, Hewlett, Bridges, Blunden, and many others since the days of William Langland. Our social historians, such as Mr and Mrs Hammond, and old Uncle Cobbett, have shown us the seamy side of that bucolic scene, the gross brutality, injustice, covert slavery, squalor, and filth. But in the bringing of those things to light, our historians have tended to neglect the positive qualities of a countryside held together by the pattern of the feudal system and the rule-of-thumb guilds. They have dismissed as superstition much of the lore of the peasant, and have failed to explain the secrets of his craft, secrets that were learned from no trade union handbook. They have neglected his personal delight

and the simplicity of his relationship with the earth
he tilled, the birds and animals he both loved and
preyed on, the flowers he sometimes trod under-
foot and sometimes set in the window of his mind,
the God he worshipped in his village churches and
objurgated in his week-day superstitions.   It was left
for the poets to record those things, and Miss Sackville-West has played a noble part in this preservation
of something which is precious, and which is
vanishing.

For whether we wish it or not, we all have to
offer our farewell, and face about to another England
that has yet to mellow for the poets of the future to
gather and convert into music, replacing our nostalgia by one for things and conditions not yet
emerged. The change, which has been gathering
speed during the past quarter of a century, has
suddenly come avalanching toward us as war-
time necessity has split our national customs. We
see at the moment agriculture and horticulture being
industrialized and mechanized; put on to a business-
like basis. It is, of course, a healthy thing to do;
but it is likely to produce a country-side which, as
well as enjoying physical comforts and urban labour-
saving devices, will be noisy with the newest ameni-
ties; the tractor, the bus, the radio, the aeroplane.

Populations and factories will be more evenly distributed. The New Forest will be loud with the mass-producing of standardized furniture, and the fields of Herefordshire with the canning of milk.

People who were born in the vanished England cannot yet acclimatize themselves to the change, and suffer from the delusion that the possibilities of bucolic poetry are dead. They cling to the past, amateur anatomists of melancholy, re-reading the autumnal songs that gather more and more mists of pathos as the world they celebrated recedes.

Miss Sackville-West is conscious that she is one of these people, and that her music represents their golden and almost enjoyable despair. In the most deep-sounding of her poems, *Sissinghurst*, she pictures herself as ' a tired swimmer in the waves of time,' moving vainly in the tides of memory:

> by birthright far from present fashion,
> As no disturber of the mirrored trance
> I move, and to the world above the waters
> Wave my incognizance.

And again, she says:

> I let a plummet down in lieu of date,
> And lose myself within a slumber,
> Submerged, elate.

Throughout her work this quality of personal elegy,

the celebration of emotions that at the time seemed inexhaustible and insurmountable, yet have been survived by her, persists as a sort of ground bass, giving a deep tone to her verse, a Roman quality which has perhaps much to do with her attraction towards the work of Virgil, and the conscious modelling of The Land on the form and mood of the Georgics. The two poems can fruitfully be studied together, and for this purpose I would recommend the recent translation of the Georgics made by Mr Cecil Day Lewis. It will be noted that Miss Sackville-West heads The Land with a quotation from the Georgics, which in Mr Day Lewis's version runs thus:

> I 'm well aware it 's hard to master this subject
>   in words
> And honour a theme so restricted.

Through that restriction of theme, however, she has mastered more than her subject. She has mastered also the waywardness and turbulence of her moods, brought down their vagueness to a precision that is hard and objective, given them a universal out of a personal value. She has put her hand to the plough in more senses than one. She says that 'the country habit has me by the heart,' and her heart, under that discipline, works the more harmoniously with her mind. This process, a hard one which cannot be mastered merely by willing, needs time, patience, and experience before it can be acquired. Once acquired, however, it produces that essential poetry which is content with simple words, unliterary associations, and humble effects. Here is an instance, from The Land:

> Now in the radiant night no men are stirring:
> The little houses sleep with shuttered panes;
> Only the hares are wakeful, loosely loping
> Along the hedges with their easy gait,
> And big loose ears, and pad-prints crossing snow;
> The ricks and trees stand silent in the moon,
> Loaded with snow, and tiny drifts from branches
> Slip to the ground in woods with sliding sigh.

It shows that she has found a new concentration of power. She is conscious of it, though in her poem she attributes it as a quality lost by the yeoman whose way of life she is describing:

> The power of being alone with earth and skies,
> Of going about a task with quietude,
> Aware at once of earth's surrounding mood
> And of an insect crawling on a stone.

That is a concise summing up of the poet's function; his universality, his particularity. It is in his gait between the two extremes, as he keeps up his lifelong traffic, fetching and carrying the references of each to the other, that we recognize him by his rhythm, and that posterity recognizes him.   Such recognition comes constantly to the reader of The Land; those moments of being surrounded by the essential self of poetry.   It is an experience impossible to account for, or to define. . One can only give examples.   It can come in a single line, as:

Some saddening of the sky before the shower,

or it can accumulate through a whole cadence, or verse paragraph, as in:

All craftsmen share a knowledge.   They have held
Reality down fluttering to a bench;
Cut wood to their own purposes; compelled
The growth of pattern with the patient shuttle;
Drained acres to a trench.
Control is theirs.   They have ignored the subtle
Release of spirit from the jail of shape.
They have been concerned with prison, not escape;
Pinioned the fact, and let the rest go free,
And out of need made inadvertent art.
All things designed to play a faithful part
Build up their plain particular poetry.

It can now be seen how she is affected by her subject.   But the fate, the environment of an artist is not the whole factor.   I doubt even if it sets the keynote of his work.   I see rather more mystery than that in the synthesis.   It is true—as Addington Symonds believed—that the artist is fettered by his period. But it is the way he wears his fetters which distinguishes him, and gives him a unique and permanent value. So with Miss Sackville-West; while we recognize the restrictions imposed upon her by place and time (and their interaction), we ultimately appreciate her for the personality which uses and pervades that predicament. For myself, I find this personality always, and in all moods (except perhaps the 'ivory tower' one), acceptable and satisfying. It has that rare quality, grace. Cowper had it in abundance. It is the secret of some likeness between these two poets. It explains why they both love quietude; why they both are gentle and grave and deliberate.

Then again I find in Miss Sackville-West an aloofness that amounts sometimes to an artificiality. I have already tried to trace the negative origin of that element in her work. But it has its effect, as it has in the work of Thomas Gray. It gives them both a sense of reserve and dignity that forbids and therefore invites approach, and touches the movement of their verse with a stateliness as in a *pavane*. This quality can carry them both over moments and moods where a more spontaneous and exalted poet would drop to a commonplace saunter. Where it goes with inspiration, it enriches it with a formality

that is regal. We know how Gray could wear the
purple. Here is an example from Miss Sackville-West:

> The owl with short and silent stroke
> Deadly to fieldfare or to mouse,
> Slants from the apple to the oak
> Across the orchard near the house:
> And through the grasses creep the small
> Creatures of twilight, hid by day;
> The snail beside the garden wall,
> The mole on his myopic way.

She can be lavish with such lines as:

> The sower with his gesture like a gift,

and

> Exalted, deathly, silent and alone.

All these examples are most characteristic of this
poet. Their technique (notice the lovely use of the
labial in the last) is an emanation of the spirit of
the person who creates it, betraying her cultural
origins, and also the very hand-touch, lips, eyes,
and hair-perfume of her spirit. As in Gray, the
aloofness, the convention, only attract attention
to the shyness they are intended to disguise. The
failure becomes one of the excellences of the poet's
style, savouring the poetic dish with a touch of
intrigue, of duplicity more innocent than naïvety
can ever be.

Such the circumstances, such the character, which

make The Land one of the most complete and beautiful
bucolics written in English.   I think that I must have
read it, sometimes to myself, sometimes aloud, at
least ten times, with the strengthened conviction
that here is poetry assured of permanence. As I
write now, once again filled with delight, I recall
the two selves of this poet, symbolized by the ivory
tower and the eight-sided tower of brick, and I see
them, in this long poem, united in a way which is
best described by a verse from a later poem:

> Never to lose, and never to forget
> Strength of initiation, gravely won,
> But through the day's incertitude and fret
> To keep this steadfast secret shared with none;
> This transcendental truth of unison
> Where we with nature, rarely tuned aright,
> Met more intensely pitched,
> Descending changed by that high symphony,
> Changed, different, enriched,
> Exalted to a faith in immortality.

After that, I can close this study of her work only
by verse of my own, a direct address to a poet who
falsely and bitterly accuses herself of being ' a damned
out-moded poet.'   I answer that as follows:

> You in your octagon, your tower,
> Searching the centuries for words
> Winged like the white and fantail birds
> Homing through air on their own power;

You in your garden where the moat
At dusk burns with reflected fire
Consuming lilies that still float
Unharmed by that remote desire
I see these ancient and these late
Devices of the soul to tell
The urgings of our tragic state,
And turn our sorrow like a bell
Whose music with ironic tongue
Shall clap the eight-sided walls with sound
Such as the Grecian Furies sung,—
Then sweetly go to English ground,
Symbol of gentleness and power,
You, in your octagon, your tower

T. S. Eliot

T. S. ELIOT: A SEARCH FOR FOUNDATIONS

The most outstanding literary excitement during the past quarter of a century is the career of T. S. Eliot. He came to Old England from New England just before the last war. His arrival was not keenly noted, for he came in the wake of another, a literary eccentric named Ezra Pound, whose verse with its exploitation of a dubious scholarship has outraged our academics and bored many lovers of poetry; myself amongst them. Nevertheless, Mr Pound has persisted. He has waged a one-man war against the English tradition, making his headquarters on Montparnasse, and using his typewriter as an erratic machine-gun.

For a few years he made quite a stir here, before crossing the Channel in disgust. Mr Eliot has believed in him, however, and remained faithful in that belief, publishing his collected poems and writing an Introduction to them, as well as dedicating his own *Waste Land* to him. It is a fidelity worth study, but not one which I would care to undertake as I lack sympathy with the subject. No just criticism comes from an assessor who begins, as I would begin, with complete antipathy. My insular taste, my delight in simplicity and a strong local tang, find no resting-place in the cosmopolitan jugglery of Mr Pound, with its pseudo-orientalism and its dabblings in medieval dialects. His verse has for me the quality of an archaeological junk shop run by a Levantine in the Tottenham Court Road.

I was not the only one who felt like this, and for some time Mr Eliot paid the penalty of his faithful association with Mr Pound. He offered his first work to a generation considerably prejudiced against him and his associations. I was guilty of that prejudice too; but there was something about Mr Eliot's early verse which alienated me. It may have been because I was a contemporary; and contemporaries tend either to adulate or suspect. I suspected; for I did not like the Pound-ism which I saw in the work. I disliked the quotations in several languages, the private or cliquish devices of telescoped images, and the parade of much literary learning. It seemed to me to be a showing off, and most un-English. It seemed to me to be the wrong way for a poet to work who wanted to settle amongst us, to skip his recent New England ancestry, and to come back to the land and customs and prejudices and deep-rooted instincts of his forefathers in this country.

That was Mr Eliot's aim as a writer. Whatever I might think of that aim, I could not see it as consistent with his literary practice, which was so emphatically unrooted, cosmopolitan, and highbrow. I, too, was young and stiff-necked, and my uncompromising attitude later caused me dismay and confusion; for shortly I met the man, and was at once impressed by a personality sincere and direct, one that bore no malice in spite of a certain constitutional acidity. I decided that I must withdraw my judgment, and await further developments.

These further developments followed rapidly; too rapidly. Mr Eliot quickly found a following of young malcontents who became an embarrassing apostolici. They imitated and magnified the qualities which I had found so puzzling. They, too, lauded Mr Pound's work. What were these qualities in Mr Eliot's early work?

I have already referred to them, and I find it difficult to discuss them more fully, because the effect reminds me too painfully of my own shortcomings and intolerance at that time. I have just re-read the poems published in 1917, and my present detachment, warmed by my deep admiration for Mr Eliot's later work, has enabled me to extract something more from them than I did twenty years ago. This

G

volume, with that published in 1920, showed the strong influence of Robert Browning. But it was Browning with a difference. It was this difference that created many of the difficulties. The other difficulties, those due to my ignorance and limited literary recognitions, I could put off by blaming the influence of Mr Pound. I can still do so, by quoting a poem written by Mr Eliot in French.

> J'erre toujours de-ci de-là
> A divers coups de tra là là
> De Damas jusqu'à Omaha.
> Je célébrai mon jour de fête
> Dans une oasis d'Afrique
> Vêtu d'une peau de girafe.

That sums up a predominating quality in Mr Eliot's work at that time; the quality of a private but bitter joke, the joke of a wanderer in strange places, the homeless man who knows not where he belongs, who sits in a Paris café amongst the other uprooted intellectuals trying to laugh off the chill of spiritual and actual exile. Perhaps the skin of a giraffe was chosen because Mr Eliot wanted to stretch his neck in order to look back across the Atlantic for a last glance at the world he had left behind, and in which he could find no place and no mission.

This homelessness, this self-sought exile was voiced

in a medium whose terse economy of structure was in itself a cynicism and a satire. That medium's obliquities of reference, its laconic asides, its broken rhythms and occasional eruptions into half-dotty dance measures, immediately caught the ear of the post-war generation. Mr Eliot became a fashion, and the rebellious undergraduates of our two blue universities began to write in his medium, airing their new, still damp learning, their youthful bewilderment at the war-quaked society into which they were growing up, their misery at their deprivation of romanticism, and their loss over the slowness of orthodox religious dogma. A whole school of poets began dancing with Mr Eliot ' round the prickly pear,' while the British public looked on sullenly, and departed. That public has not yet come back, and poets still have to write for each other; a hungry audience, reluctant to pay.

The Mr Eliot of that time, as I have suggested, was not the fully self-discovered poet. I think that the work which made him fashionable was still apprentice work. He was still articled to Browning. But he went more than one better than his master. He speeded up the dramatic impersonations, quick-changing at such a lightning pace that within the range of a few poetic images he put himself beneath

the skin of half a dozen characters. Look at the first
poem in his volume of Collected Poems, The Love
Song of J. Alfred Prufrock. See how it begins, with
Browning's hurried, hearty method setting the scene,
followed by a sudden recoil, a denial of that assump-
tion of heartiness as the underlying acute sensibility
of the poet reveals itself and at the same time uncon-
sciously explains the initial affectation of man-of-the-
wordliness.

> Let us go then, you and I,
> When the evening is spread out against the skv
> Like a patient etherized upon a table;
> Let us go, through certain half-deserted streets,
> The muttering retreats
> Of restless nights in one-night cheap hotels
> And sawdust restaurants with oyster-shells:
> Streets that follow like a tedious argument
> Of insidious intent
> To lead you to an overwhelming question. . . .
> Oh, do not ask, ' What is it? '
> Let us go and make our visit.

And we do make that visit. It is a searching one.
It goes to inquire into the practice and incidence of
sexual love, of friendship, of all human relationship
as tossed and derided by the events of a post-war
society. It brings out the potential personality of

the poet, and shows hints of his intense nervous emotional make-up, an organism so susceptible to the contact of daily life and ultra-daily life, that he has had, hitherto, to assume this armour of a steely cold intellectualism; this bright, flashing scholarship carried from far, unhappy Boston and polished on Montparnasse.

So much for the Browningesque scene. There is not much solidity or quietness about it. There is much that is over-display, as there was in Browning. As for the idiom, Mr Pound's influence appears, just as Leigh Hunt's vulgarisms appeared in Keats's early work. But already there is this pronunciation of self, and in 1922 it emerges with a touch of authoritativeness. Mr Eliot is no longer afraid of his quick - change impersonations. Within the first twenty-five lines of The Waste Land he has been a multitude of folk. He starts with a blast of Walt Whitman's trumpet, announcing that

> April is the cruellest month, breeding
> Lilacs out of the dead land, mixing
> Memory and desire, stirring
> Dull roots with spring rain.

But immediately we are taken to a castle in central Europe, our sex is changed, someone, a relative, calls

us ' Marie ' warningly, and before we have assimi-
lated this metamorphosis, we are thrown amongst

> A heap of broken images, where the sun beats,
> And the dead tree gives no shelter, the cricket no
>   relief,
> And the dry stone no sound of water.

From that time onward, and in spite of Mr Eliot's
promise that ' I will show you something different,'
the journey in his Proteus-like company is a journey
in spiritual deserts, where the cactus, the prickly pear,
the waterless rock, the dry rattle as he shakes several
desiccated literatures, build up the *mise en scène*.
For many years during Mr Eliot's still unpronounced
quest, this landscape is a constant. It is dry and
dusty, but the dust is that of history. It is the scene
which Shelley looked on when he wrote the sonnet
Ozymandias. It contains the rocks to which Shelley
chained his Prometheus. That being so, I have
always been puzzled by Mr Eliot's loud-spoken dis-
like for Shelley's genius. Is it the irritability of one
traveller towards another? However, we begin to
know where we are with Mr Eliot. He is wearing
through the brilliancy, the parade of scholarship, the
Poundisms. We see a figure somewhat grim, sardonic, twitchingly sensitive, and prepared for an
asceticism which has not yet been fully assumed.

This is the poet who introduces us to his world, with the words:

> This is the dead land
> This is cactus land
> Here the stone images
> Are raised, here they receive
> The supplication of a dead man's hand
> Under the twinkle of a fading star.

It means that he is coming to the frontier of this world of intellectual and social sophistication. He is shaking off his embarrassment of followers, those imitators who, in deifying him, have sought to fix him on a pedestal, an unwilling Simeon. He is within sight of another country.

Once having glimpsed that country, he does not look back. The vision acts upon him with astonishing results. It is rather as though he had been on the road to Damascus, and had met with Saul's blinding experience there. His work is seared, too, by that experience It burns away almost to nothing. Poking about amongst the mental and emotional ashes, we see one recurrent phrase sticking out, clean as a burned bone:

> Death's other kingdom.

It is a bleak phrase. What does it mean? what is its full significance? All that follows in Mr Eliot's career as poet—and maybe also as man—is a commentary upon that phrase.   It is not an easy process, although it is a simplifying one.   As he sings in his more recent poem, *East Coker*:

> Home is where one starts from.   As we grow older
> The world becomes stranger, the pattern more
>   complicated
> Of dead and living.   Not the intense moment
> Isolated, with no before and after,
> But a lifetime burning in every moment
> And not the lifetime of one man only
> But of old stones that cannot be deciphered.

Earlier in the same poem is a passage which reveals, with nobility, and an intensity now characteristic of all his work, much more of the meaning of that reference to death's other kingdom.

> In order to arrive there,
> To arrive where you are, to get from where you
>   are not,
> You must go by a way wherein there is no ecstasy.
> In order to arrive at what you do not know
> You must go by a way which is the way of
>   ignorance.
> In order to possess what you do not possess
> You must go by the way of dispossession.
> In order to arrive at what you are not
> You must go through the way in which you are not.
> And what you do not know is the only thing you know
> And what you own is what you do not own
> And where you are is where you are not.

We see that it is a difficult country, still stony,
still with its vegetation spined and arid. But there
is something more. Some illumination, some purpose, has given this lonely traveller a direction, a
path amongst the stones and the cactus. He is
finding something. He is finding a country which
he recognizes as his own, the native land of his
second birth, that more important birth to which
he refers again and again in his later poems. ' Except
ye be born again.' And at the end of The Journey
of the Magi:

I had seen birth and death.
But had thought they were different; this Birth was
Hard and bitter agony for us, like Death, our death.
We returned to our places, these Kingdoms,
But no longer at ease here, in the old dispensation.
With an alien people clutching their gods.
I should be glad of another death.

All this period of discovery is marked by an intense agony of soul. The poet is finding that his
early life, with its uneasy groping after a congenial
setting in a continent other than the one in which
he was born, was nothing but a physical rehearsal
of the journey which later was to bring him to self-
knowledge, and the comforting humility set therein.
But that comfort is not yet.

I have been wounded in a war of phantoms,

says the hero in his recent play *The Family Reunion*,
and this same person, his spokesman, speaks directly
of the processes which are assailing the poet who
has now thrown away all his past assets of success,
his followers, his flashy scholarship, and his hard
American wit.

> The sudden solitude in a crowded desert
> In a thick smoke, many creatures moving
> Without direction, for no direction
> Leads anywhere but round and round in that
>   vapour—
> Without purpose, and without principle of
>   conduct
> In flickering intervals of light and darkness;
> The partial anaesthesia of suffering without
>   feeling
> And partial observation of one's own automatism
> While the slow stain sinks deeper through the
>   skin
> Tainting the flesh and discolouring the bone—

Note that echo from the Shelley whom he once
so hated; the Shelley who in *Adonais* was moving into
a world of light Dantesque in tone, singing:

> From the contagion of the world's slow stain
> He is secure. . . .

Note, too, something in Eliot that is Dantesque;

that is, the rhythmical lilt of unaccented syllables
(those indexes of the *temperature* of a man's soul) in
most of his later work, and notably in this new play.
Re-read that passage above and see how he has draped
the material of syllables about the four-stress line.
Note the ease of it, the grace of gesture, and the fall
of the material about the bones, the skeleton. Such
work is the sign of a spirit revived and reassured, as
was Dante's in *Paradiso.*

There is much I should like to analyse; the re-
newed contacts with society and individuals now
that the poet has found a firm footing. You will
see his shrewdness confirmed by tolerance, and his
wit made genial with sheer fun. You will see also
a further purgation of spirit as he tries to re-read his
past in the light of this new assurance.

For us, there is only the trying. The rest is not
our business.

In that trying, all possibility of complacence is
consumed, and he still experiences

a lifetime burning in every moment
And not the lifetime of one man only
But of old stones that cannot be deciphered.

He finds
only a limited value
In the knowledge derived from experience.

The knowledge imposes a pattern, and falsifies,
For the pattern is new in every moment
And every moment is a new and shocking
Valuation of all we have been.

We see the agony of personal uncertainty, of
diffidence, of almost crushing humility, still present
in his work. But how different in effect and expression from that malaise of his youth! Now it leads
him to purer and purer candour in his work, instead
of to a camouflage of book knowledge and picturesque
bitterness. What bitterness is left is something that
bites to the bone, and is directed upon his own
inadequacy in his new world, ' death's dream
kingdom,' instead of upon the banality of twentieth-
century Europe and America.

With all this characteristic dryness, elements of
his nature which are as ineradicable as his physical
make-up, we see him passing into his inheritance,
a rare one which more comfort-loving folk would
not like to share. But it has a beauty which few
poets reach; a morning-of-the-world quality of light
and simplicity, like the Giotto illustrations of
Dante's world, where

> beyond the hawthorn blossom and a pasture
> scene
The broadbacked figure drest in blue and green
Enchanted the maytime with an ancient flute.

Blown hair is sweet, brown hair over the mouth
  blown,
Lilac and brown hair;
Distraction, music of the flute, stops and steps of
  the mind over the third stair,
Fading, fading; strength beyond hope and despair
Climbing the third stair.

Such is the world in which he has set his founda-
tions, or rather discovered them. Knowing his own
place there, all the latent geniality, tolerance, and
simple virtue of his nature are revealed, both to
himself and to the human society which he no
longer lashes because of its sordidness and stupidity.
His present stance is that of a happy warrior, home
at last, and we can leave him where

  Under a juniper-tree the bones sang, scattered and
    shining
  We are glad to be scattered, we did little good to
    each other,
  Under a tree in the cool of the day, with the
    blessing of sand,
  Forgetting themselves and each other, united
  In the quiet of the desert. This is the land which ye
  Shall divide by lot. And neither division nor unity
  Matters. This is the land. We have our in-
    heritance.

ROBERT GRAVES: A TRAVELLER IN THE DESERT

What Harold Munro did for English poetry during
the two decades from 1912 has still to be put on
record. The appreciation would not be a small one.
Amongst other valuable service, he published Robert
Graves's first book, *Over the Brazier*, in 1916, while
the young poet, twenty-one years old, was on
active service in France. Not much notice was
taken of the book, although the boom in poetry,
consequent upon Rupert Brooke's romantic death, had
already begun.

A year later, *Fairies and Fusiliers* appeared, with
another publisher, at the same time as Robert
Nichols's *Faun's Holiday*, and the two poets began to
be talked about as literary twins. Time quickly
sorts out these chance relationships. It was not
long before Robert Graves commanded singular attention. I recall a conversation which took place in
1919, soon after the armistice, when an earthly
paradise was being built at Versailles. Roger Ingpen
had just started a small publishing business, and he
and I were eating boiled eggs in W. H. Davies's
dusty rooms in Great Russell Street. Davies had a

shrewd instinct for new voices. I, a youngster then, listened reverently as he and Ingpen discussed the the author of *Fairies and Fusiliers*. I remember one sentence exactly as it was uttered by Ingpen. He was a pale, ghost-like man, hesitant and absent-minded, and usually spoke with his eyes half-shut as though the sound of his own voice were shattering his nerves. His emphasis at that moment was therefore the more startling. He said: ' I believe Graves has the most perfect technique of any poet of his generation. He will survive most of them.'

That was good prophecy. I do not hesitate to take it up, twenty years further along the corridor of time, and augment it with this recollection, and another shout of my own. For ever since that day, when I was introduced to Graves's work, I have not failed to find delight in it, and to watch its development.

That development, while not being inconsistent, has been devious, and in many respects disconcerting. Graves has published nineteen books of verse in all, and from them he made a volume, which he called *Collected Poems*, in 1938. In a preface, he explained why that collection was so austere. He found that during a period, after his marriage, he wrote verse most of which he has not cared to reprint. 'Poetry to me at this time,' he said in his preface, 'was neither a formal muse nor a familiar deity, but a hidden Janus (one head benignant, the other malevolent) whose unpredictable behaviour made the poet's task an impossible one.'

Having come to this impasse, he set out to find the cause of it. This task caused him to throw out, as side-lines, a series of studies in technique and literary history: On English Poetry, Poetic Unreason, Another Future of Poetry, Contemporary Techniques of Poetry. 'This preoccupation,' he said further, 'led me to a study of psychology; I was searching for some means of capturing and holding the reader's attention by hypnotic suggestion. I tended to make the test of a poem's worth not its internal coherence and truthfulness but its power to charm a large audience. Equally misguided was my recourse to philosophy to justify such poetic practice.' The mere names of those books, together with his concluding remarks, show with what seriousness and curiosity this poet was watching himself and his work, and puzzling his mind to find out the truth of the relationship between the two. He went further than that, however, and in this further inquiry he was a forerunner of the generation which followed him, and to a large extent ignored him; the generation of

Robert Graves

Auden, Day Lewis, Spender, and others, whose technique is slight, and whose theory of living is dogmatic and puerile, in comparison with those of Robert Graves.

Concluding his discussion of his own efforts towards a full consciousness of what he had been doing and what he was likely still to do, he said: ' My essays on the psychology of poems gained wide currency and have done corresponding mischief.' And turning from this introspective purpose to a more ethical one, he said: 'In 1925 I first became acquainted with the poems and critical work of Laura Riding, and in 1926 with herself; and slowly began to revise my whole attitude to poetry.'

That revision is one which the critic to-day cannot freely examine without intruding upon privacies and personal relationships only hinted at by the poet here and in his famous prose autobiography, *Good-bye to All That*. Perhaps in fifty years another critic will not be so restricted, and will be able to ' chatter about Harriet ' at great length, and win applause thereby. I doubt if he will get near the truth, for it is a truth which is still eluding the poet himself, and will for ever elude him. We think we discover the heart of our purposes and impulses. We sit and brood, especially in our middle years, the

H

strange noontide years of inaction, but the process is as futile as that of an onion which should endeavour to skin itself.

What influence Graves received at this time is incalculable. It is also temporary, for, as I shall try to show from his work, I believe that he is a creature who walks alone, though he is horrified by the solitude; and that his temperament will force him to do so until the end of the journey. Again and again he betrays a personality that cannot learn the technique of social relationships; one that is never restrained, even by painful experiences, to the necessary reserves, defensiveness, caution, business aplomb, diplomacy, or whatever we may care to call the procedure by which men and women make their way in the world. This perpetual innocence is a sign of the true poet. It may not be a virtue. Indeed, often it is the source of those obliquities of conduct and contact which make poets talked of as being feline, unreliable, irresponsible. Both Keats and W. B. Yeats have had much to say about this. In Yeats's own personality it often took the form of a deliberate malice, which in his old age broke out in a magnificent gesture of savagery and revolt, crystallizing into some of his finest verse.

What is so odd is, that this detachment usually

is interrupted by periods of close, child-like dependence, either upon another individual, or upon some
social acclamation, or both. The lives of Shelley
and Browning will at once give examples of what I
mean. The alternative give and take of these two
extremes of the poet's temperament create much of
the material which feeds his work, because he illus-
trates the conflict in terms of the struggles which
he observes, objectively, in the world outside himself. In spite of his detachment, he has to exercise
his highly sharpened consciousness. Robert Graves
has not been an exception. In the following concluding passage of his preface, he shows how he
acknowledges these two manifestations of temporary
dependence.

That the proportion of what would be called
'unpleasant poems' is so high in this twenty-three-
year sequence surprised me on first looking it over.
But I see this now not as a furious reaction against
the anodynic tradition of poetry in which I was
educated, but as the blurted confession of a naturally
sanguine temperament: that the age into which I
was born, in spite of its enjoyable lavishness of
entertainment, has been intellectually and morally
in perfect confusion. To manifest poetic faith by a
close and energetic study of the disgusting, the con-
temptible and the evil is not very far in the direction
of poetic serenity, but it has been the behaviour most

natural to a man of my physical and literary inheri-
tances. Other steps remain, and a few have already
been taken. I should say that my health as a poet
lies in my mistrust of the comfortable point-of-rest.
Certainly, this suspicious habit, this dwelling upon
discomfort and terror, has brought me good luck:
for in the midst of my obstinate stumblings there
have come sudden flashes of grace and knowledge—

> As to the common brute it falls
> To see real miracles
> And howl with irksome joy.

I have to thank Laura Riding for her constructive
and detailed criticism of my poems in various
stages of composition—a generosity from which
so many contemporary poets besides myself have
benefited.

That passage, generous in its candour, offers many
points for critical speculation. It contains the whole
argument upon which the later comers, to whom I
have already referred, have based their poetry and
its political affiliations. It reveals how fully aware
this poet is of his own disposition. It defines the
history of his fight and emancipation, and hints at
the truth that, indeed, poetry in its essence is always
a demonstration of personal growth, of hope either
furthered or frustrated, and is therefore ' the blurted
confession of a naturally sanguine temperament ' as

distinct from the guile and cynicism of the man of
the world.

Finally, and here it touches upon the qualities
which make Robert Graves distinctive, it describes
his self-immolatory nature, his determination to put
away this native independence and detachment, and
to take a god here, and another there, who shall
demand from him a discipline of ' suspicious habit,
and dwelling upon discomfort and terror ' which in
the end shall be a hair-garment means towards salva-
tion through ' grace and knowledge.' I believe it
is a gesture indicative of greatness; of that purity of
spirit without which no lasting poetry is written.

I would emphasize that it is not this discipline
which makes him unique. For all poets must have
a hero, a mentor; possibly to do their thinking for
them, while they are concerned with the agony of
translating that thought into the words which shall
be more sensuous than flesh and more mysterious
than blood. In the history of poets' lives and inspiration, we see the most incongruous loyalties of
this kind: Dante walking between Aquinas and Virgil,
Shelley between Plato and William Godwin, Yeats
between Madame Blavatsky and any old Celtic guy.
In the course of his revelations, Robert Graves is
explicit upon his particular loyalties; and in his last

one, the one which he claims to have set him on
the road at last to a right self-knowledge and a right
and healthy relationship with human society, he has
expressed himself in some of the most original and
beautiful of his verse. In the poem To Whom Else?
for example, he salutes his 'sovereign muse' as
patiently as any old-fashioned love poet.

> To whom else other than,
> To whom else not of man
> Yet in human state,
> Standing neither in stead
> Of self nor idle godhead,
> Should I, man in man bounded.
> Myself dedicate?
>
> To whom else momently,
> To whom else endlessly,
> But to you, I?
> To you who only,
> To you who mercilessly,
> To you who lovingly,
> Plucked out the lie?
>
> To whom else less acquaint,
> To whom else without taint
> Of death, death-true?
> With great astonishment
> Thankfully I consent
> To my estrangement
> From me in you.

That is an odd piece; but its full meaning is rich
and various. This 'plucking out of the lie,' this
'consent to estrangement'; these are experiences that
reach down to the deeps of this poet's nature, a
process that tortures him, that turns his past into a
new-living present with a double agony.   In a group
of fourteen such poems, whose technical affiliations
are deliberate in subservience as the poet humbles
himself in this dreadful devotion, he pays his tribute.
He describes his old literary comradeships with
fellow writers, his war-time memories, prides,
horrors, and ambitions.

> This was to praise ourselves, rebuke ourselves
> How we sufficed, fell short, exceeded
> In days before you came, you first,
> Who plucked the speech-thread from a jargon-tangled
> Fleece of a thousand tongues, wills, voices,
> To be a single speech, twisted fine;
> Snapping it short like Fate then—
> ' Thus much, no more—'
>
> And we confessed that since you came
> We might no longer feign and stutter
> As poets of the passionate chance,
> Nor claim the indulgence of the hour.
> Our tongues must prompter be than those
> That wag with modish lamentation—
> Or lost men, otherwise, and renegades
> To our confession, maudlin-sane must die
> Suicides on the stair of yesterday.

Mr Graves's development as a poet has been litered with his suicides. From each he has sprung to a new life—but the same poet has survived!

Who is that poet? What is he? I have called him a traveller in the desert, because I have seen his progress as a painful, thirsty one, in which he struggles from one influence, one oasis, to another, remaining with each until his thirst is quenched and his strength restored, and then driving on again with his own obstinate daemon for camel.

It is in these periods of solitary progress that he speaks most authentically, and reveals the nature which no influence can change. It is one beset by fear, in the same way that a child is, or that Blake was. Huge powers, of good and evil, come at his imagination. Many of his poems are simple articulations of this terror. Here is an instance. But notice how skilfully it is clothed; how the repetition is drummed in with an effect like that of African drums.

Nobody, ancient mischief, nobody,
Harasses always with an absent body.

Nobody coming up the road, nobody,
Like a tall man in a dark cloak, nobody.

Nobody about the house, nobody,
Like children creeping up the stairs, nobody.

Nobody anywhere in the garden, nobody,
Like a young girl quiet with needlework, nobody.

Nobody coming, nobody, not yet here,
Incessantly welcomed by the wakeful ear.

Until this nobody shall consent to die
Under his curse must every man lie—

The curse of his jealousy, of his grief and fright,
Of sudden rape and murder screamed in the night.

It is the drive of this primitive fear that has furthered his experiments in technique. Nothing is so reassuring to a frightened man as a bag of tools. It gives him the assurance that he will be able to get out, of any predicament into which the mystery of the future may slam him, with a groaning of locks. It fortifies the poet, who is always, waking and sleeping, driven by this obsession, always possessed of this ' dernière innocence et dernière timidité,' as Arthur Rimbaud described it in his *Saison en Enfer*. This tension between innocence and timidity can be recognized at once as Mr Graves's ' blurted confession of a naturally sanguine temperament.'

Every poet comes to it at some period in his life; and usually it comes during those mysterious decades,

the thirties and forties, when youth is dying, and
the full, authoritative man is being born as a result
of that youth's self-squanderings upon the lovely
body of life itself, the ever-feminine power of
experience. The more violent this death, the more
agonizing this rebirth, the firmer is the poet's
technique, and the more personal and original his
idiom. Mr Graves's work proves this relationship.
So quick, so highly nervous has been his sensibility,
that his work seemed from the beginning to foreshadow the later experiences of his life. It was as
though the poet made the man, while the man was
making the. poet; a paradoxical reciprocity. Look,
for example, at this early poem, Lost Love. Note the
already close, hard imagery, and compare this with
the more symbolical imagery of his later poems.
Except for the ripened scope of the images in the
later work, their angle of vision is the same, and
their manner of employment identical; another proof
that the poet, in spite of his changes of theory, and
his several monitors, has remained true to himself.

> His eyes are quickened so with grief,
> He can watch a grass or leaf
> Every instant grow; he can
> Clearly through a flint wall see
> Or watch the startled spirit flee
> From the throat of a dead man.

Across two counties he can hear
And catch your words before you speak.
The woodlouse or the maggot's weak
Clamour rings in his sad ear,
And noise so slight it would surpass
Credence—drinking sound of grass,
Worm talk, clashing jaws of moth
Chumbling holes in cloth;
The groan of ants who undertake
Gigantic loads for honour's sake
(Their sinews creak, their breath comes thin);
Whir of spiders when they spin,
And minute whispering, mumbling, sighs
Of idle grubs and butterflies.
      This man is quickened so with grief,
He wanders god-like or like thief
Inside and out, below, above,
Without relief seeking lost love.

But the process of enriching those images with a
fuller symbolism has been one of agony and a
suffering that has driven this poet mercilessly, on
the one hand to a ceaseless self-examination, and on
the other to sharper and sharper experiment in his
medium of verse forms. Striving to recognize his
own symptoms, he has gathered into his imagination a store of historical pryings that have over-
flowed into his prose work, notably the two *Claudius*
tales. But he has not found an explanation in the
past. He has turned to the contemporary scene,

experimenting as Mr Eliot has done, in the reaction from the sordid, non-significant details outside the back door of civilization. He finds in everyday actuality a hell presided over by a devil who

> ieads the sick words into parliament
> To rule a dustbin world with deep-sleep phrases.

Amongst those reactions is the mood of satire, in which he uses his wit with a penetrating relentlessness to further mental and spiritual inquiry, so that every gust of his laughter is a most pertinent question, pressing home the problem until it becomes a fresh torture, and another range of self-discipline and self-discovery. No matter how he may dramatize that process, it remains to torment him.

> To the galleys, thief, and sweat your soul out
> With strong tugging under the curled whips,
> That there your thievishness may find full play.
> Whereas, before, you stole rings, flowers and
>   watches,
> Oaths, jests and proverbs,
> Yet paid for bed and board like an honest man,
> This shall be entire thiefdom: you shall steal
> Sleep from chain-galling, diet from sour crusts,
> Comradeship from the damned, the ten - year -
>   chained—
> And, more than this, the excuse for life itself
> From a boat steered toward battles not your own.

A poet who can promise himself such a life as that is one prepared to make the final renunciation, in order that his work may be purged of dross, and burned down to a bone-clean simplicity. That is what Mr Graves claims to have done, and I think that his poetry will remain for Time to justify that claim.